Waterford Whispers News
2023

COLM WILLIAMSON

Gill Books

Gill Books
Hume Avenue
Park West
Dublin 12
www.gillbooks.ie

Gill Books is an imprint of M.H. Gill & Co.

9780717197248

Designed by seagulls.net
Copy-edited by Catherine Gough
Proofread by Adam Brophy
Printed and bound by Białostockie Zakłady Graficzne S.A, Poland

Waterford Whispers News is a satirical newspaper and comedy website published
by Waterford Whispers News. Waterford Whispers News uses invented names in
all the stories in this book, except in cases when public figures are being satirised.
Any other use of real names is accidental and coincidental.

For permission to reproduce photographs, the author and publisher gratefully acknowledge the
following: © Adobe: 4B 5, 6, 13B, 16B, 18, 20, 23, 28B, 28T, 29, 30, 31B, 32, 35T, 35B, 36T, 36B,
39, 40T, 40B, 45T, 45B, 46T, 46B, 48, 49B, 50, 52T, 52B, 53, 54B, 56T, 56B, 57, 59B, 60T, 60B, 62,
63T, 65, 66, 69, 70, 73B, 85L, 89T, 91B, 92, 93T, 97T, 98TL, 100TL, 101T, 101B, 102, 103, 104T,
104B, 105, 106, 107B, 107BC, 108B, 109, 110, 111, 113T, 113B, 115TR, 115B, 112, 114, 116,
117, 118T, 119, 120, 121T, 121B, 122, 123, 124T, 124B, 125CR, 126CL, 128, 129B, 130T, 130B,
131, 134, 135B, 136B, 139T, 140, 142T, 143T, 143B, 145, 148B, 149, 150, 151T, 154, 157, 158,
160, 161, 162, 163, 164, 165, 166, 168, 167, 170, 172; © Alamy: 12, 13T, 15L, 17R, 21T, 21B, 25,
31T, 34, 38B, 43, 44BL, 47, 61, 63B, 67, 68, 71B, 75, 86, 88, 95, 96, 136T, 138, 142TC, 148BR;
© CBS Photo Archive/Getty Images: 24R; © Ciaran 'Yohan' Brennan: 14, 38, 90; © Colm
Williamson: 146, 147, 152TR; © Davis Ramos/Getty Images: 14; © Gareth Chaney/Collins: 38CR;
© Houses of the Oireachtas/Wikimedia Commons: 74; © iStock: 11, 15R, 41, 49T, 51, 91L,
108T, 112C, 152T, 153, 159; © Library of Congress/Wikimedia Commons: 58CR; © Mgreason/
Wikimedia Commons: 58CL; © NurPhoto/Getty Images: 38CL; © Sam Boal/rollingnews.ie: 38TC;
© Samuraiantiqueworld/Wikimedia Commons: 72BR; © Shutterstock: 4T, 7T, 8, 9, 10T, 10B, 12,
16T, 17L, 19, 22, 24L, 33, 37, 42, 44B, 47, 54R, 59T, 64T, 64B, 71T, 72B, 73B, 76, 78T, 78B,
79, 80, 81T, 81B, 82T, 82B, 83, 84, 85R, 87, 89B, 93B, 94, 97R, 98T, 100T, 115TL, 118B, 125C,
126C, 129T, 132T, 132B, 133, 135T, 144, 151B, 156, 160TL, 160TC, 160TR, 169, 171; © Sinn
Féin/Wikimedia Commons: 26; © Sportsfile/Getty Images: 137, 139B; © Store norske leksikon/
Wikimedia Commons: 58R; © United States Department of Justice/Wikimedia Commons: 58L.

The author and publisher have made every effort to trace all copyright holders,
but if any have been inadvertently overlooked we would be pleased to make
the necessary arrangement at the first opportunity.

The paper used in this book comes from the wood pulp of sustainably managed forests.

A CIP catalogue record for this book is available from the British Library.

5 4 3 2 1

CONTENTS

ABOUT THE AUTHOR

Colm Williamson created *Waterford Whispers News* in 2009 when he was made unemployed during the financial crash. Though it began as a hobby, with Colm sharing stories with family and friends, his unique brand of topical, distinctly Irish satire quickly attracted thousands of fans. Now *Waterford Whispers News* has over 670,000 followers on Facebook, 246,000 on Twitter, 184,000 on Instagram and 45,000 on TikTok as well as an average of four million page views on the website every month. *WWN* has performed live shows everywhere from LA to the 3Arena. Accolades include being banned from RTÉ before it was cool after the last appearance sparked protests and over 6,000 complaints from the public. Colm runs *Waterford Whispers News* from his home town of Tramore in County Waterford.

LETTER FROM THE EDITOR

Dear readers,

It is my sincere wish that *WWN*'s dear readers enjoy this book that my staff worked tirelessly to produce. Don't forget to buy the exclusive €450,000 NFTs (remember them?) which accompany it.

I have been assured that this book contains several pictures and at least four paragraphs of writing (double spaced) but, rather than celebrate this titanic achievement, my mind turns to those less fortunate, those who continue to struggle in an Ireland deaf to their sufferings.

This year has been tough for many people. More than anything, it has been a harrowing case of the haves and the have nots.

TV personalities asked to hand back money, construction firms begging cap in hand for the government to pay invoices for €1.7bn in additional hospital-building costs while, on the other hand, the Irish public had energy credit payments and bonus Fuel Allowance, Disability Allowance, Child Benefit and Carer's Support Grant payments rain down on them like confetti shot from a magic money canon.

Poor man's feast, rich man's famine.

It has never been harder to be a rich man or a rich man's wife in Ireland than in 2023. Just because I am a Maltese resident for tax purposes doesn't mean I don't have a soul!

I ask you, when oh when will the Irish wealth creators and visionaries catch a break? Such is the fast pace of today's world, you'd nearly forget that landlords like myself had to endure four horrible months of not being able to evict people in 2023.

Waiting until 1 April to lift the ban? Now there's a joke if I ever heard one.

The government was happy to bail out the public because they don't have the cop on to put on a hoodie at home when they're cold, but when have the rich ever received a bailout?

What happens when a smart sensible businessman like myself, having overextended himself by borrowing heavily to expand his property portfolio, has to meet repayments at exorbitant interest rates? When will the one per cent catch a break?

Apologies, I know this serves as a newspaper column of sorts and not a place for me to air my grievances, but I just don't feel up to penning my usual column targeting refugees and the LGBTQ community.

Yours factually,

Bill Badbody,

Temporary Deputy Editor, Chairman of the Irish Landlord League, Philanthropist, Trutharian and Entrepreneur.

ww news

Waterford Whispers News

POLITICS

UNEMPLOYMENT

DOZENS OF LILT MEN MADE REDUNDANT

THERE go the Lilt men. Lilt!

Lilt, it had a totally tropical taste, pineapple and grapefruit in it, and has now been discontinued after 48 years leaving dozens of Caribbean drivers across the world redundant.

'Wagwan?' asked one former Lilt man at a protest over redundancy packages outside Leinster House today, where Lilt trucks brought traffic to a standstill causing huge delays across Dublin city centre. 'I've been delivering Lilt for the past 30 years and now where am I supposed to work? All I know is Lilt. Lilt was everything for me. Lilt. Hot sun is bright. Lilt.'

The tangy drink began in 1975 with the strap line 'The Totally Tropical Taste', and it was only sold in Ireland, the UK, Gibraltar and the Seychelles, creating jobs for thousands of Lilt drivers who started work early to deliver cans of Lilt directly to people's homes before they went to work, which eventually sparked a three-year war with milk men in '87 over territory.

'Yes, the deaths of over 5,000 milk and Lilt men was the beginning of the end for all home Lilt and milk deliveries,' explained Lilt man and war veteran Kyle Johnson. 'The demand for deliveries wasn't the same after that, but we still had muck savages ordering Lilt in places like the west of Ireland.'

'It was only a matter of time before Big Soda bought them out,' stated large bottle of Cidona delivery man, James Roche, who was made redundant in the mid-nineties after a new law was introduced banning under 18s from pubs past 9 p.m.

EVERYONE GETTING RODE TO FUCK, FINDS LATEST ESRI REPORT

PEOPLE from all reaches of society are being 'rode to fuck', a new report from the Economic and Social Research Institute (ESRI) has found.

The new research suggests that everyone is being gouged left, right and centre, with no end in sight to being rode into oblivion like some kind of paraplegic bunny stuck headfirst in a warren.

'Energy companies are riding you, fuel companies are riding you, hotels are riding you, bars are riding you, shops are riding you, landlords are riding you, banks are riding you, even your own government is riding you, and all you can do is sit there and let them rip your behind open until all your intestines flop out onto the floor in a steaming pile of gloop,' the report states.

The report pinpointed that the working and middle classes were getting far more action than those in the higher tier, the latter of which seemingly doing most of the riding while swinging one hand in the air

like a rodeo cowboy, shouting 'Yee haaw' with every thrust of their throbbing member.

Commenting on the report, author Mark Tracey said: 'People should find solace in the fact that everyone is being unwillingly bent over and shafted equally by the same group of profiteers at the top of the chain, so that's something to note.' He concluded, 'Dare I say we're all being rode together?'

HOUSING

'LET THEM SLEEP IN TENTS'

FACED with a torrent of news stories featuring people describing the toll the lifting of the eviction ban will have on their lives, chief amongst them homelessness, Taoiseach Leo Varadkar mused from a Leinster House balcony that those facing life in the doorway of a shop should simply avail of a tent.

'Not just any tent, the glamping ones you get at festivals, they're great,' advised the Taoiseach, who sometimes fretted about the disastrous outcomes people would face were they subjected to the tyrannical rule of a Sinn Féin-led government.

'Or failing that, have you seen those great, big, luxury tents they use in the Sahara desert for tourists? How much could they cost, €50?'

While his comments drew accusations that he, along with his coalition leaders, couldn't be more out of touch with the plight of the many people struggling to find accommodation, the Taoiseach insisted those assertions were incorrect.

'A quick glance at Eamon Ryan's latest tweets would show you that his mind is firmly on how fecking brilliant China is and how it's a must visit for everyone, including people crying as they desperately search Daft,' added the Taoiseach.

Now fanning himself as he is hand-fed grapes by Micheál Martin, the Taoiseach continued to provide calming and reassuring words for the public.

'Let them have "hostels", let them have "additional measures", let them have "can't solve this overnight", let them have "safety nets", let them have "housing coming on-stream any day now",' the Taoiseach bellowed.

Elsewhere, ESB announced profits of €847 million, much to the relief of the government who can now use an energy windfall tax to pay for €800 million worth of new tax breaks for landlords.

Predictions for 2024

The world will shock itself at how quickly it forgets about the ongoing instability in Sudan.

HOUSING

'WE DIDN'T TAKE EVICTION DECISION LIGHTLY,' TD TELLS LANDLORD MATES IN CLUBHOUSE AFTER 18 HOLES

'HEART'S broken, could hardly sleep, sure. To duff that chip off the green when I was in with a shout of a birdie and then do it again today, haunted I am. This will gnaw away at me,' confirmed coalition TD Noel Abhaile to his mates as they reviewed their round of golf.

'Oh, how am I sleeping what with the eviction ban ending? Didn't take the decision lightly, took it bloody quick though, wha'? Hahaha,' chuckled Abhaile, who has successfully skipped paying for his round by going to the toilet.

Abhaile is believed to be just one of dozens of TDs who will be stern of face this weekend when talking to fellow landlords about how tough the decision was to end the eviction ban.

'But seriously lads, hand on heart now – tell me, be honest. No one I've talked to here at the club has any issue with the ban ending, same down the yacht club, what about you lads? I'm starting to think all this homeless stuff is a bit overblown, like Drico's drive on the 4th. Hiyooo, I'm on fire,' Abhaile said, the weight of thousands of evictions clearly pressing down on him.

'The only thing worse than lifting an eviction ban before having any plan in place was that bunker shot on 13, wha'? Sorry, I'm repeating jokes now. No new jokes, no new policies, says

> **'The only thing worse than lifting an eviction ban before having any plan in place was that bunker shot on 13'**

you,' Abhaile added, just glad to be able to destress after a tough week.

'And it's like you said, Billo, "market forces", what alternatives were there? None, if you don't include the hundreds put forward by housing charities, academics, industry experts and the opposition. Our hands were tied – by you lot, haha! Bloody wouldn't stop begging me to lift it. Well, you can all lift the cards out of your wallets and get the next round in.'

BIDEN'S VISIT: THE HIGHLIGHTS

TAKING in Belfast, Dundalk, Dublin and Ballina, it's been quite a visit for US President Joe Biden. Here are some of the highlights from an action-packed few days, which have been truly unforgettable.

'Where's my fucking petrol station and service station named after me? Bidenplaza now or I fucking riot!' a visibly annoyed Biden said, pitching a bitch-fit five minutes after landing on the island.

A controlled explosion of Arlene Foster's rage was carried out as she reacted to Biden's strong support for the Good Friday Agreement and the Windsor Framework.

Biden drew criticism for flying in on a modified jet, which bore the words 'Air Force Taig'.

Thinking he was suffering from auditory hallucinations, Biden could be seen asking his handlers if his water had been spiked after hearing the Louth accent.

Biden called news that The Coronas would play at his Ballina address 'a declaration of war'.

'I don't care if I have official engagements, cancel them; I want to go to Air Bound Trampoline Park in Dundalk,' Biden barked at his aides.

Greeting Leo Varadkar on the tarmac of Dublin Airport, a misty-eyed Biden reflected, 'What a transformation Ireland has undergone. To think when my ancestors fled Ireland it was a country captured by an entitled class who locked people out of land ownership.'

Biden's Secret Service detail worked up an estimated €2 million bill for Supermacs in under 24 hours.

Several Secret Service men have pledged to leave their families back home after being bewitched by Dundalk's many beauties.

The Minister for Finance Michael McGrath directly OK'd handing over whatever money it takes to reopen the Amber nightclub after Biden, who was planning to hit it up, was devastated to hear it had closed.

Irish and international media were admitted to hospital and treated for exhaustion after searching out and finding a record number of the most gombeen motherfuckers imaginable to interview on live TV.

Fearing questions about the unforgivable failure that was the botched withdrawal from Afghanistan, among other thorny issues, Biden faced tough-ball slap downs such as, 'How great is Ireland on a scale of 10 to 10?' from the assembled media.

Unruly and possibly tipsy, President Biden was heard to loudly threaten Spirit Store bouncers with a precision drone strike after he was refused entry by bouncers because he was wearing Crocs.

Other memorable moments include when Biden:

- Attended the ribbon-cutting ceremony for the new 50ft gold statue depicting Rob Kearney defeating the Black and Tans.
- Lost the White House in a game of cards in The Cot & Cobble in Ballina.
- Said 'Mayo For Sam' – the secret signal to set off a dozen nuclear arms against anyone who stands in the way of the Mayo football team.

TECHNOLOGY

GOVERNMENT UNVEILS DONKEY DYNAMOS TO TACKLE ENERGY SHORTFALL

OVER 400 donkey dynamos are to be erected nationwide in a bid to secure energy supply due to the significant risks to the country's electricity network, the government announced today.

Coaxed to walk in circles by a dangling carrot on a stick, shift-working donkeys attached to a large dynamo are expected to inject enough power back into the national grid to charge a Nokia 3210 in just under eight hours.

'This clean source of energy ... ah, shite,' Eamon Ryan began, just as he accidentally stepped in donkey manure. 'Excuse me. This clean source of energy is sustainable and doesn't rely on fossil fuels,' he said, now demonstrating by walking around in circles ahead of a concept donkey dynamo in County Louth today. 'Obviously we may need tens of thousands of these to curtail the current crisis, but this government is confident we're on the right track.'

Asked whether he took carbon emissions from the donkeys into account, Mr Ryan deflected the question, instead pointing out that there were a few snags in the plan, but reconfirming it was a plan, nonetheless.

'Yeah, well, we could attach balloon-type bags to their rears to capture whatever flatulence is emitted by the donkeys and then let them float into space,' he retorted, seemingly chuffed with his quick thinking. 'Obviously this is at the early stages of development, but let's try to be optimistic when it comes to fighting climate change; there's far too much pessimism from the media in this regard,' he concluded, as the donkey ironically stopped for a dump and a little standing-up nap.

Council Notices

Waterford Council has called for anyone partaking in the indiscriminate dumping of rubbish to do so in Kilkenny.

HOW NORTHERN IRELAND IS ALREADY CHANGING NOW UNIONISTS ARE A MINORITY

WITH THE 2021 Northern Ireland census results revealing that Catholics make up a larger percentage of the population, the Unionist minority is already seeing instantaneous and sobering changes.

Having spent the day in the six counties, *WWN* saw firsthand some of these astonishing changes, which included:

- For the first time since 1921 the majority of toasters in Northern Ireland are no longer kept in the cupboard.
- Now that they are officially a minority, there are very subtle initial signs that Unionists are developing a persecution complex.
- NHS waiting lists have disappeared.
- A number of Union Jacks have faded overnight, like they were a picture in *Back to the Future*.
- Stormont is up and running again.
- Currently seeking help in the A&E department, the DUP's Jeffrey Donaldson woke up speaking fluent Irish.
- The 0.06% of the population who are Welsh have made a shocking attempt at a power grab.
- Protestants have already begun unwittingly consuming Communion wafers, which have been sneaked into their breakfasts.
- With 29% of people in Northern Ireland identifying as 'Irish Only' and a significant majority of 71% of people identifying as other designations in the census, Sinn Féin will ignore this and continue insisting on a border poll tomorrow.
- The Good Friday Agreement has been renamed the Comhaontú Aoine an Chéasta.
- Londonderry? Never heard of it.
- Thousands of Unionists are contemplating having sex with their wives for the first time in years in a bid to get the birth rate up.
- It has been announced next year's Orange marches will take place in Lough Neagh.

HOUSING

MINISTER FOR HOUSING APOLOGISES AFTER ERROR SEES 700 MODULAR GNOMES BUILT

HEAPING embarrassment upon a bonfire of failures, Housing Minister Darragh O'Brien has been forced to apologise over the construction of 700 modular gnomes.

'Someone in my department's typo was missed and the tender was sent out with modular gnomes instead of modular homes,' O'Brien told a gathering of refugees.

'But on the plus side, we've got you all some lovely, colourful gnomes. Look at this one, he's great, ha! Feel free to name him "Darragh",' added the minister, speaking nearly a year after the government pledged and failed to build 700 homes for Ukrainian families.

'The optimist in me says I see tearful children here small enough to actually fit inside some of the gnomes, so technically we've delivered a home.'

The delivery of the gnomes slowed down somewhat after concerned locals formed a blockade around the kiln that was used to make the gnomes.

Placards reading 'Go Gnome' and 'We Must Gnouse Our Own First' were seen amongst the crowd.

'In terms of any protests, even for the most brazen element of xenophobia, we will endeavour to politely ask them to stop harassing refugees, and once they don't listen to us we intend to capitulate to their every demand,' said a spokesperson for the government's making-the-problem-worse team.

GAVISCON DISCLAIMER STATES IT CAN'T HELP YOU STOMACH THIS GOVERNMENT

THE makers of Gaviscon have been forced to include small print on their packaging to make it clear that neither their liquid nor chewable products can prevent a sinking feeling in your stomach every time the government makes a new announcement.

Gaviscon is one of the more popular medications in Ireland due to our excessively high heartburn rates, brought on by our frequent feeds of Guinness and our inability to eat meals at a normal, human rate.

However, there have recently been a number of complaints from consumers who were upset that the milky antacid offered no relief from discomfort caused by government policy, forcing a change to the label to prevent confusion going forward.

'This product will NOT change your ability to stomach this government,' reads the new warning. 'You will still feel the same churning sensation when you hear about lucrative government contracts given to businesses for a service the State should provide itself.

'You will still experience nausea when the homeless figures are released every year, and you will still be sick to your stomach when you hear about yet another TD who "forgot" to declare their rental properties. Note: No amount of Gaviscon can help you in these matters.'

Although Gaviscon is useless when it comes to the government, a new product called 'voting' is said to offer some relief.

CRIME

CRIMINAL ASSETS BUREAU SEIZES €12BN FROM DEPARTMENT OF HEALTH IN PROBE INTO ILLEGAL NURSING HOME CHARGES

IN THE LARGEST seizure of cash in the history of the Irish police force, the Criminal Assets Bureau (CAB) has taken possession of €12 billion from the Department of Health, which it is believed the department had been withholding under false pretences, as the money made up the compensation owed to individuals illegally overcharged by the State in public nursing home fees.

'This money is clearly from the proceeds of organised fraud and wanton crime and illegality. The idiots even left a paper trail,' said one CAB official, drawing up a list of suspects consisting of former Taoisigh and ministers for health who had knowledge of the plot.

Sealed in evidence bags and placed on display in the same manner as the seizure of .00005 grams of cannabis, the €12 billion will now be returned to vulnerable families the State actively plotted against to conceal the fact they were entitled to compensation after subjecting them to illegal nursing home charges.

'This is classic criminal cartel behaviour: conceal your misdeeds and tell no one,' said one CAB official on learning that the State knew it was at fault and couldn't win cases taken to court, so instead pursued a strategy of dragging out and prolonging legal challenges while also keeping settlements from being publicly reported so as not to attract attention.

Asked if this strategy was designed to ensure poorer families without the means to pursue legal action were shut out from receiving compensation they were 100% entitled to, a spokesperson for the Department of Lack of Accountability said, 'Duh! Of fucking course. We've got an Einstein over here!'

Meanwhile, gardaí interested in pursuing this matter have been told to contact whistleblower Shane Corr.

> **'This money is clearly from the proceeds of organised fraud and wanton crime and illegality. The idiots even left a paper trail'**

Things We've Learned as a Nation

With improvements in roads and all the new bypasses, it's no longer a long way to Tipperary.

BREAKING ━━━━━━━━━━━━━━━━━━━━━━

HAMMERED TAOISEACH WILDLY SWINGS PUNCHES AT BIDEN BEFORE BEING SUBDUED BY SECURITY IN TRADITIONAL ST PATRICK'S EVENT

FILLED with hooch after abstaining from food since his arrival, Taoiseach Leo Varadkar was led into the White House this afternoon as part of a traditional Saint Patrick's event acted out every year since the founding of the state, *WWN* reports.

Uttering profanities at staff and those in attendance, Mr Biden gave the Taoiseach the traditional nod, before the blind-drunk Irish leader was faced towards the 80-year-old president and threw a flurry of punches.

'Put 'em up, sonny,' the American president taunted, his sleeves now rolled up and fists poised vertically like an early-twentieth-century boxer. 'You'll have to do better than that if you want to hit me, me laddie,' he added, as security casually intervened to sounds of applause from those attending the event.

Now puking into a bin, the exhausted Taoiseach was shown to his quarters to get some rest ahead of his remaining visit.

'Ah, they don't make them like they used to,' a shadowboxing Biden jeered, referring to the days of old when Irish and American leaders would actually engage in a traditional 'fisticuffs' fight in the Oval Office to mark the beginning of the Saint Patrick's Day celebrations in Washington. 'I'm old enough to remember FDR and Dev at it, when men were men and black eyes were standard.'

A vestige from a bygone era, the punch-up isn't the only poorly aged tradition maintained by the nations, as both leaders continue to pretend the US Army doesn't use Shannon Airport as a taxi rank before carrying out war crimes.

The annual fisticuffs duel was reduced to an event of mere pageantry post-1962, after JFK was knocked clean out with a spinning right hook from then Taoiseach Seán Lemass, causing a severe concussion and requiring 134 stitches.

EU PARLIAMENT

MICK WALLACE CRITICISES THANOS BUT INSISTS WEST IS NO BETTER

IRISH MEP Mick Wallace has made headlines once again for his contributions in EU parliament as he qualified his criticism of evil super-villain Thanos by stating that the West isn't innocent in all this.

'Absolutely, I've no problem saying it, I've said it in the past and I'll say it now: Thanos shouldn't have snapped his fingers and erased 50% of the world's population,' Wallace said as part of a speech in the EU, as the chamber debated imposing sanctions against Thanos and his coterie of murderous lackeys.

'But at the same time, there's some people here in the West who have some cheek criticising Thanos with a straight face when you look at their colonial and imperial history and illegal wars,' added Wallace, upbraiding fellow members of parliament.

'I was as sad as anyone to see Spider-Man reduced to ashes, the lad was only a young fella, but the Avengers have intergalactic blood on their hands so I'll keep calling out hypocrisy when I see it.'

Wallace's comment has come under scrutiny after reports re-emerged from eight years ago concerning the time the Wexford politician was part of an election monitoring group on planet Zorbarphina 8, which saw Thanos win 99% of votes in a referendum asking, 'Do you want Thanos to blow up your planet while you are all still on it?'

YES, TD OBJECTED TO HOUSING IN AREA, BUT HE CAN EXPLAIN

AN OPPOSITION TD has been forced to defend himself after it was discovered he objected to 5,403,789 units of eight-bedroom houses, which

would have come to market for the princely sum of €12.

'What this country needs is suitable sustainable housing, which this is. But then the thing is, I was made aware that locals would vote me out if I supported it, so I rejected planning permission to erect a backbone,' explained the TD, who is picking his pension over the public good every time, no contest.

Citing the fact that this development would not be built by the ghost of James Connolly's moustache, the Labour Party added its name to a growing list of objectors that would be asking for a gold medal if they were the ones to first back such a housing scheme.

'Don't let the government pull a fast one on you, these houses are perfect

Bill's Political Tips

Get friendly with developers and property investment funds so that when you lose your seat after failing to solve any of the housing issues, you'll get a cushy job lobbying for firms trying to make money off said issues.

for a number of families and single people, but if they built enough of these our poll numbers would suffer and we need the housing crisis to go on until the next election at the very least,' explained a Sinn Féin spokesperson.

BAREFACED

CORRUPTION

LEAKED INTERNAL AN BORD PLEANÁLA REPORT RECEIVES THREE BERTIES ON CORRUPTION SCALE

THE UNIVERSAL unit of measurement for corruption recognised by all Irish people, the Bertie Scale of Corruption (BSOC), has measured the contents of a leaked internal An Bord Pleanála report at 'three Berties' in severity, with the public reacting in shock as the full weight of the continuing scandal finally hit home.

'Some still use the imperial measurement system, which puts this scandal at about 1.2 Haugheys, but I think the Bertie Scale is familiar to younger folks,' one corruption expert said. 'Especially when it comes to giving evasive answers, ducking accountability and just generally

being up to their necks in dodgy shenanigans,' they added of an internal report, which the Minister for Housing has sat on since November and refused to make public.

The internal report, leaked by *The Ditch* website, shows clear instances of board members interfering with the independent work of planning inspectors and instructing them to make material changes to reports to the benefit of property developers, in many instances insisting these instructions be 'off the record'.

'At three Berties, it would suggest there's a good chance everyone at risk of consequences will be scrambling in the background to ensure this is

> **'Some still use the imperial measurement system, which puts this scandal at about 1.2 Haugheys'**

a case of "rigorous tribunal in the public interest" rather than "evidence passed to Gardaí, see you in the criminal courts",' explained one expert in accountability in Ireland.

However, the expert warned that regardless of where a scandal lands on the scale, be it 1 or 10, the results remain the same.

'Any reasonable person might call such brazen acts "corruption", but what we've learned from the Bertie scale is that no matter where it lands it can be dismissed as "management failures", "a misunderstanding" or "corporate governance concerns", and all involved can move on to another cushy gig.'

HOUSING

SINN FÉIN CONFIRM TIRELESS FIGHT FOR TENANTS DOESN'T INCLUDE ITS DIRECTOR OF FINANCE'S TENANTS

'WE are a proud Nationalist party, fighting for the working people, but at the same time we're really loose on those things when it comes to our own Director of Finance,' confirmed Sinn Féin today after *The Ditch* revealed Sinn Féin's Des Mackin was the sort of landlord all other bastard landlords aspire to be.

Illegally converting an office into a substandard apartment that has insufficient ventilation, and renting out the home he purchased from the council at a 50% discount despite an agreement stipulating he could not do so, Mackin is exactly the sort of law-flouting, money-grabbing landlord Sinn Féin claims it has no time for.

'Hang on now a second, he's our Director of Finance, it's not like these

are things to do with lacking integrity on matters of finance,' added a Sinn Féin spokesperson of Mackin, who was the director of a company forced into making a €40,000 settlement with Revenue over under-declaring its tax liabilities.

'You're acting like saying "no comment" and "it's a private matter" makes us some sort of hypocritical, spineless party devoid of morals.'

Elsewhere, several Sinn Féin supporters were treated for 'scorched vocal cords' after repeatedly screaming 'Typical media stitch-up'.

'OK, now that is a real disgrace, and typical of an out-of-touch elitist party putting profit over people,' a Sinn Féin spokesperson said when presented with the exact same

scenario, but with the party changed to 'Fine Gael'.

WWN then asked if the party had any comment on the fact they are under SIPO investigation for declaring an election spend of €313,000 in their 2016 accounts, but telling SIPO they only spent €76,000.

'Anywho, did you hear Mary Lou McHusband is suing that thundering disgrace Shane Ross?' confirmed the party.

POPULAR [RESTAURANT NAME HERE] CLOSES AFTER [YEARS IN BUSINESS HERE]

THE hugely popular [Restaurant Name Here] in [Location Here] has sadly announced its closure today after [Years in Business Here], *WWN* has learned.

Owner [Proprietor Name Here] cited the increase in energy bills and produce costs along with government inaction as the reasons for the closure, and thanked all their customers who supported them over the years.

[Sad image of owners with staff who will all be bombarded with threatening social welfare letters to get a job in a few weeks.]

[Emotional quote from café/bar/restaurant/shop owner outlining how the government watched on as a whole galaxy of financial hurdles continually tripped up any progress the business could make since scraping through Covid lockdowns with peanuts aid before ruthless revenue sheriffs moved in and took all their kitchen equipment so they couldn't even operate anymore.]

[Restaurant Name Here] is one of thousands of businesses folding thanks to [Blame inflation caused by the war in Ukraine or whatever bullshit narrative it is at the time of writing here].

Meanwhile, [end with some good news about an Aldi or a Wetherspoons opening in the area to balance out the article so local politicians don't get on our case saying we're biased when it comes to accurate reporting].

NORTHERN IRELND

PSNI RESPONDS TO SCENE OF DUP HOLDING NORTHERN IRELAND HOSTAGE

AS REPORTS indicate that the DUP is once again proving a barrier to a breakthrough in negotiations on the Northern Ireland Protocol, the PSNI is responding to the scene of Northern Ireland being held hostage.

'Demands remain unclear, something about making everyone agree the earth is 6,000 years old, over,' one officer said, radioing back to the station after reaching the scene.

'Viable explosive-verbal-diarrhoea device found on the face of one Sammy Wilson,' confirmed another

officer assessing the situation, which has seen the DUP looking for any excuse to prevent Stormont returning to regular operations.

Holding an empty stapler to his head and warning he would shoot himself, Jeffrey Donaldson insisted he was 'serious' and would pull the trigger unless a man called Rishi Sunak confirmed Northern Ireland's economy would stop out-performing the rest of the UK.

'This isn't fair, we're British like you … well, not you specifically,

Rishi, obviously. But we're British like the rest of Britain … well, except when it comes to matters like access to abortion, but we don't want to be any different from the mainland … well, except when it comes to LGBT "rights",' rambled Donaldson.

The DUP then threatened Sunak with performing 'seven tests'.

'And if you and this deal pass the seven tests, then we'll make up more tests because if it wasn't clear yet we've no intention of ending this "holding Northern Ireland hostage" thing,' added Donaldson, before asking the PSNI for an emergency delivery of 4,000 Union Jacks when officers offered them food.

Council Notices

Council seeking racists for participation in new study on local hobbies.

TAX

REVENUE SHAKING DOWN SMES FOR WAREHOUSED TAX LIKE SOME KIND OF MEXICAN DRUG CARTEL

A COUNTY Waterford businessman is being treated for PTSD today after being shaken down by Revenue henchmen over warehoused tax from the Covid lockdown period, when he was forced to halt all operations by the government, with the same government now instructing bailiffs to act like drug dealers owed a debt.

'Where's our fucking money, you piece of shit,' one Revenue letter read to the businessman, parking all niceties and getting straight to the point. 'If you don't fucking pay us, we'll take everything your business owns and then fuck any future of owning another business, OK?'

Mark Sharpe, who operates a restaurant, had to warehouse his VAT liability due to having to close his business for 18 months, before then opening to a new round of being rode left, right and centre by a series of increasing costs, including inflation, wage hikes, new bank holidays, hikes in VAT, gas, electricity and whatever you're having yourself.

'First it was the threatening letters and then the knocks on the door from the Sheriff threatening to take the very bit of equipment I use to make the money that will eventually pay them if they just backed off a bit,' Sharpe explained, who will now have to make some kind of

> ## 'We're Revenue and we make drug cartels look like Mary-fucking-Poppins'

payment arrangement with the Revenue cartel despite knowing he'll never be able to pay it.

'They said they'll let me pay it back over the next year with 3% interest, but if I fail that, which I certainly will along with half the bloody country, they'll fold me like an origamist on crack – oh, they're so fucking generous. If only I was a multinational, I'd never have to worry about any of this.'

The shakedowns have rattled thousands of businesses around the country in the hopes of retrieving the VAT owed to Revenue, despite Revenue admitting to already making up for the Covid Exchequer shortfall, opting instead to make thousands of

Irish businesses fold over a forced debt by the State.

'We're Revenue and we make drug cartels look like Mary-fucking-Poppins,' Revenue replied when asked about the recent barrage of threats, intimidation and their blatant bastardness, concluding in a New York mob accent, 'Oh, you have quadruple energy costs – fuck you, pay us. Oh, the cost of everything has doubled – fuck you, pay us. Oh, it's all our fault for putting you in this position in the first place – fuck you, pay us.'

TECHNOLOGY

LIST OF TOWNS IRELAND'S POWER GRID CAN SACRIFICE FOR DATA CENTRES

FOLLOWING news that TikTok is to build another energy-hogging data centre in Ireland, the government has published a list of towns the national grid can sacrifice so that the Chinese-run multinational can freely process everyone's data.

'At the current growth of data centres here, we will need to allocate 30% of Ireland's entire national grid to power these servers, which is enough to power every single residential home in Ireland – so sacrifices will have to be made,' Minister for the Environment and Green Party leader Eamon Ryan explained.

'We have shortlisted a number of towns across the country which we feel can do without electricity so that the Chinese government can store every click, location ping, finger scroll, facial gesture and eye movement you and your children make when using the app,' he added. 'If the Amish communities in the US can do it, then so can you.'

'The towns we've earmarked for the energy sacrifices are Moate, Carrick-on-Suir, Clonmel, Athy, Portarlington, Drogheda, Callan, Castleblayney, Enniscorthy, New Ross, Tipperary Town, Bunclody, Longford – basically anywhere this government and its predecessors have ignored over the past few decades and left rot into a drug-infested, social-welfare-dependent hell-hole laden with crime and poor mental health services.'

Mr Ryan suggested the news isn't all bad for those living in these towns, saying that new career opportunities will be generated from the electricity embargoes.

'Just think of all the great jobs this will create, like candle makers, horse and cart builders,' he continued, without so much as a blink of an eye. 'Carbon emissions will be way down – it will be great for the local environment while we simultaneously clean up on fining these data centre companies for misusing everyone's data.'

Dictionary Additions of 2024

'**C.E.Yo.**': the greeting your boss gives you in the morning (not to be confused with C.E.Blow. – when your boss is off his face on coke at the Christmas party and hits you in the face, but you can't really do anything about it because you need this job and nobody saw him do it so it's just easier to forget about it).

TECHNOLOGY

DATA CENTRE GRANTED PLANNING FOR MOHER CLIFF FACE

AN BORD Pleanála has granted permission for the first of nine data centres to be constructed on the side of the Cliffs of Moher, which will benefit from the cliff's cold temperatures and damp atmosphere to help keep vital data for multinational companies cool, *WWN* has learned.

'You won't even notice them, and the best thing is they won't rely on the country's water supply to keep cool and will use the strong winds to power themselves, which is a

win-win for everyone,' insisted a Department of Environment source today at an unveiling of the plans for the new centres.

It is understood the first centre will focus on housing specific data from Chinese social network TikTok, to harbour the increasing number of Andrew Tate videos which have swarmed the site in the last few months.

'Due to the high increase of Tate videos, we've had to expand our data servers and we believe the Cliffs of Moher data centre to be the perfect location to deal

with such a large cache of video files,' a TikTok spokesperson revealed.

Aptly named the Tate Centre, the construction of the building has been branded an abomination by the local tourist board, claiming that the construction will be unsightly and will deter visitors from visiting the site.

'For fuck's sake, lads. A data centre on the side of the Cliffs of Moher? What gobshite thought this would

be a good idea?' a brief statement from Clare tourism board read today, welcoming the news.

> **'For fuck's sake, lads. A data centre on the side of the Cliffs of Moher? What gobshite thought this would be a good idea?'**

Quotes of The Year 66

'Tough shit to anyone who had me in their dead pool. Later, losers!'
– Stevie Wonder

CORRUPTION

NIALL COLLINS REALLY OUT-FIANNA FÁILING HIMSELF THIS TIME

JUST WHEN you thought he couldn't possibly out-Fianna Fáil himself any more, party junior minister and ex-county councillor Niall/Neil/Noel/ 'whatever he's naming himself this week' Collins has managed to break the party mould, *WWN* has learned.

'Bertie was even impressed,' a party source began. 'We thought Collins' previous alleged misdeeds over planning submissions using various different names was FF 101, but he appears to have gone one further when he voted as a councillor to sell council-owned land that his own bloody wife went on to buy. Who, by the way, is now trying to sell five social housing units from the site

back to the same council for a very tidy sum – totally out-Fianna Fáiling themselves.'

Voting on the land sale and failing to declare a conflict of interest is a criminal offence according to the Local Government Act 2001, and it carries a potential two-year prison sentence. Due to this fact, the news is expected to make the party's wall of corruption fame, joining a list too long to mention, as we'd be here all day writing them.

'It's the most Fianna Fáilest thing I've ever heard,' boasted another party member. 'Just when you thought our corruption era peaked, on comes Niall, knocking it out of the illegally acquired, rezoned park.'

Commenting on the news reports that one of his party members is embroiled in a corruption scandal, Tánaiste Micheál Martin defended Collins by stating 'Sinn Féin, Sinn Féin, Sinn Féin' as his face turned red.

THE SINN FÉIN SUPPORTER'S GUIDE TO REACTING TO NEGATIVE MEDIA COVERAGE

IT'S the well-worn, predictable and pathetic tactic played out day in, day out in the media and online, but just how should dyed-in-the-wool Sinn Féin supporters react to having their party besmirched?

Prepare for cynical swipes, blatant defamation and harmless enough observations with this indispensable guide:

- Behave as you would expect someone to behave after finding out a nemesis pissed in their cornflakes, regardless of the severity of the perceived slight.
- Faint in the style of a Victorian lady whose corset was tied too tight.

- Was the criticism or polite inquiry in any way legitimate? Did it come from someone you know would sooner stick their mickey in a blender than vote for the coalition parties? Not possible. Time to faint again.
- Everything is a shadowy conspiracy which the media executes in unison in a calculated and clandestine

manner. But don't say it in such a way that you look like a deranged conspiracy loon; this is the real type of conspiracy. 'They got to you too, didn't they?' strikes the right note when responding to someone who says something incendiary about the party's stance on postage stamps.
- Petition the Oxford Dictionary to replace the definition of 'infallible' with 'Sinn Féin'.
- Sometimes it's important to admit you were wrong – in this case, admit you were wrong in thinking the party's critics couldn't sink any lower.

Predictions for 2024

Elon Musk deletes his Twitter. As in, all of Twitter.

COALITION LATEST

GOVERNMENT HITS NEW HEIGHTS BY FUCKING OVER NURSING HOME PATIENTS, MOTHER AND BABY HOME SURVIVORS, AND DISABLED PEOPLE IN ONE WEEK

THE COALITION government has hit new, dizzying heights of 'surely this will collapse the government?' comments this week after unveiling plans to exclude 24,000 survivors of Mother and Baby Homes from a redress scheme because, hey, they probably haven't suffered enough trauma in their lives.

Coupled with doubling down on their defence of an indefensible legal strategy that saw every effort made to ensure people illegally charged for stays in public nursing homes didn't get the compensation they are entitled to, there is a risk the government have used up their Bastard Behaviour Quota for the year … and it's only the start of February.

'Don't forget it was official State policy to rob 12,000 people with disabilities of welfare payments they 100% qualified for, and it only came to light because RTÉ uncovered it,' said one Fine Gael member, who pointed out that the subsequent cover-up wasn't their fault because it was presided over by Fianna Fáil in 2009, a party they're happy to share every day in government with.

WWN was under the impression it would be incredibly hard to get government TDs to defend myriad acts of moral bankruptcy, but no, TDs were only too happy to excuse it all.

'Well, it really comes down to whether you think it's correct that we exclude 24,000 people from the Mother and Baby Home redress even

> **'Just as well we're beyond feeling shame and the public just take it lying down or we'd all resign'**

though they were ripped from their mother/child, or whether you have an actual soul,' confirmed a Green TD, who says foregoing human decency balances out in the long run because we have a few electric buses now.

'And hey, we're not done yet: there's a British inquiry into the Omagh bombing we might not aid or comply with in any way, and then there's some ignoring of masked men being cheered on as they suggest burning refugees out of their accommodation to do, too. Just as well we're beyond feeling shame and the public just take it lying down or we'd all resign,' concluded one Fianna Fáil TD.

TECHNOLOGY

FIANNA FÁIL UNVEILS NEW CRYPTO BROWN ENVELOPES

CONSTANTLY evolving to keep up with the times, the Republican party Fianna Fáil have launched a new range of crypto-based brown envelopes called 'The Bertie', *WWN* has learned.

The new digital wallet for politicians will feature end-to-end encrypted security features allowing donors, bribers and gangsters to secretly transfer money in a bid to get political favours without any of the risk, making it a hot favourite among the party.

'The problem with brown envelopes is they're very bulky and, well, brown,' a party source explained. 'Many of our members would have had to wear ill-fitting suits to hide envelopes in the

past, but with the new Bertie wallet we can store thousands, even millions in our pockets without having to own a bank account.'

Much like a Fine Gael WhatsApp group under investigation, or a Garda Commissioner's phone, the digital wallet has a 'delete all' feature for when a government inquiry or a tribunal is launched.

'All the bribes are kept on a secure cloud for later retrieval,' the source added. 'We expect this to revolutionise the political landscape,

Bill's Political Tips

Falsely claim responsibility for every new development in your area with a social media post beginning, 'Delighted to announce ...'. This will lead people to believe you made it all happen.

Quotes of The Year ❝

'I've listened carefully to all the lovely encouragement from the Irish public and so, yes, I WILL run for president.'
– Bertie Ahern

with property developers and business lobbyists already scrambling to sign up for The Bertie.'

The launch of the new wallet is expected to see a surge in property developments across the country.

HOUSING

'HE'S AN INTERGALACTIC EEJIT': MILES O'BRIEN DISOWNS HOUSING MINISTER BROTHER

DARRAGH O'BRIEN had just minutes to enjoy surviving his 80th vote of no confidence motion of the year in the Dáil before his estranged brother, Starfleet Chief Petty Officer Miles O'Brien, broke his silence on his sibling's political career.

'I've travelled the galaxy and seen countless alien races of distinct variations, ideologies and capabilities, but it's safe to say Darragh can't be beaten for aimless eejitry,' Miles said in an interview with Deep Space FM.

Miles spoke of how he frequently feels like it is impossible to escape the inept shadow of his brother.

'There's not a bar or hovel I enter in the known galaxy where it's not brought up. There's a race of space fish with snails for hair – four billion miles from Earth – who were slagging me over him. Sniggering and whispering under their water, "There's your man with the brother who doesn't know what a house is",' said Miles, visibly peeved.

> '**There's your man with the brother who doesn't know what a house is**'

'Listen, I've no time for the Klingons, but sweet merciful Christ even they don't try to sell "11,500 people homeless" as "we're making progress",' Miles offered.

Miles went on to explain his difficult childhood with Darragh, who would periodically swallow LEGO pieces instead of building anything with them. When Miles played dress-up as an astronaut, Darragh would dress in a suit and sit behind a desk doing nothing for what seemed like years.

'Do you know what this absolute liúdramán of an empty shite wrote on my birthday card last year? May the force be with you! "Live short and rot," says I to him. That peeved me more than the refusing to get the State to build social and affordable housing.'

BERTIE AHERN CONFIRMS HE WHOLEHEARTEDLY ACCEPTS APOLOGY FROM IRISH PEOPLE

AFTER being asked by assembled media if he needed to 'rehabilitate' his image upon his re-entry into Fianna Fáil and Irish political life, Bertie Ahern confirmed that he accepts the Irish public's apology for how they wronged him.

'I wholeheartedly accept the apology. It was very moving to see the crowds line the streets and cheer "Bertie for president",' explained

Council Notices

Council can confirm the completion of 200 social housing units at McCormick Park. Psych! Only joking, build-to-rent all the way.

Ahern, mistaking a warm reception at a small Fianna Fáil party event attended by craven invertebrates who care only about their own self-advancement and bank balance for being representative of the entirety of Ireland.

Footage of the stomach-turning event has caused many to vomit uncontrollably as they watched the enthusiastic round of applause received by the disgraced politician.

'It was very gracious if a little late,' Ahern said, humbled by what he hallucinated as a sincere and

> ## 'Even the cribbers and moaners offered to wash my feet by way of apology'

lengthy apology by the nation, which included flowers.

Asked again if being labelled as among the most malign and corrupt influences in Irish politics in the last half century would hamper him in any way, Ahern responded, 'I agree, it's rare a whole nation apologises to someone they've wronged, but even the cribbers and moaners offered to wash my feet by way of apology.'

Elsewhere, the public continue to ask Fianna Fáil, 'Are you serious with this bullshit? Is this a prank?'

THINGS MORE OFFENSIVE THAN EOIN Ó BROIN'S TWEET

THE Sinn Féin TD (Terribly Disrespectful) Eoin Ó Broin shared artist Mála Spíosraí's image depicting present-day gardaí attending and aiding a Famine-era eviction.

While several Fine Gael TDs were treated for shock in the country's private hospitals, some genuinely unhinged people with clear agendas tried to claim the following items were more offensive than art containing social commentary.

- That time Dublin City Council JCB'd a homeless man to near death and that was the last thing you ever heard about the matter.
- The fact actual, real and illegal evictions are taking place.
- The fact Ireland having 11,742 homeless people is not receiving anywhere near the same kind of criticism as a tweet of a picture.
- Darragh O'Brien's haircut.
- Lobbyists for property developers begging the government to change the law so they can shrink garden sizes, reduce natural light in apartments and reduce fire safety standards in new builds.
- Vast swathes of TDs concealing the fact they are landlords, with some lying on planning permissions.
- People saying Guinness 0.0 tastes just like Guinness.
- The time survivors of the Carrickmines fire, which killed 11 people, all members of the Travelling Community, had their temporary site for re-accommodation objected to and blocked by local residents.
- Pensioners receiving eviction notices.

- Gardaí never intervening when an illegal eviction is taking place.
- Sinn Féin's Director of Finance Des Mackin illegally converting office space into 'wholly substandard' apartments in which windows couldn't be opened.
- Nineties clothes being back in fashion.
- In 2021, 17 out of 31 councils not bothering to enforce and collect the vacant sites levy.
- Families affected by mica being ignored by the government when they point out the shortsighted and easily fixed flaws in the redress scheme.
- People dismissing the musical legacy of the Sugababes.
- Landlords evicting tenants claiming they are 'moving in a relative', only for tenants to find the property listed as one of 16,000 active Airbnbs which are required to be registered, but compliance for this is literally at 0%. And the fact there will be no consequences for this.
- *Intermission* still not getting the respect it deserves as one of the all-time great movies.
- Two-thirds of apartments and duplex homes built over three decades having significant defects.
- That five years on from the setting-up of the Land Development Agency, it says it might get 5,000 homes built in the next decade, hard to tell.
- NAMA.
- Any result that comes up from a simple 'Garda controversies' search on Google.
- Crocs.

WW news

Waterford Whispers News

LOCAL NEWS

CRIME

'IS IT TOO LATE TO RETRACT MY STATEMENT?' JONATHAN DOWDALL ASKS

'SERIOUSLY, this isn't how it played out in the film *Goodfellas*,' a worried-looking Jonathan Dowdall began. 'Is it too late to retract my statement, like I can just pretend I lied again and everything will be OK?' he added, while looking through a plastic surgery catalogue for a new face.

Frantically flicking from page to page, looking for the most unrecognisable appearance and contemplating a sex change, Dowdall's confidence in the Irish witness protection programme was fading fast as his former pal The Monk was found not guilty of murdering gangland rival, David Byrne.

'If the Irish judicial system can fuck up this badly, what are my chances as a State rat surviving on the outside? I mean, these fucking idiots will probably relocate me next door

to Gerry Hutch's gaff in Lanzarote,' said the former Sinn Féin councillor, his lips quivering with the fear of karma coming back to waterboard him.

Dowdall, previously convicted with his father of falsely imprisoning and threatening to kill a man, was also charged for facilitating the killing of David Byrne with Mr Hutch, before turning on him in exchange for a lighter sentence and a glitzy State witness tag.

'In *Goodfellas* your man Henry went on to live a full and fruitful life after ratting the mob out to the Feds, but I fear I'm going to get more of a Joe Pesci in *Casino* ending in a corn field somewhere being hammered with baseball bats,' Dowdall concluded, before opting for the African female option in the plastic surgery catalogue.

MOTHER KNEW IT WASN'T SON IN 'HI MUM' WHATSAPP MESSAGE SCAM AS THE LITTLE PRICK NEVER TEXTS

THE latest phishing scam attempting to retrieve victims' financial information through a new 'Hi Mum' WhatsApp text message wasn't fooling one Irish mother this week, who stated she knew straightaway it wasn't her 'prick of a son' because he never contacts her, *WWN* reports.

'I got excited for about three milliseconds before copping on that Niall would never text me like that,' Geraldine Roche recalls the moment she received the suspicious WhatsApp. 'He certainly wouldn't start with a "Hi Mum",' she added. 'If they had texted me "Give us a lend of 200 quid, Ma, will ya?" then maybe I would have fallen for it, but this is some amateur hour bullshit

right here … fucking "Hi Mum" me arse.'

Only seeing her son at Christmas due to the fact he lives 20 kilometres down the road, Mrs Roche advised fellow mothers that if something is too good to be true, then it probably is.

'Firstly, if he was stuck for money, you'd be sure as the day is long he'd be on your doorstep looking for it and not pussyfooting around with some elaborate niceties through WhatsApp,' she went on. 'It would be too easy to refuse him money through text messages and he knows that, the little shit.'

It is understood the scam was a second attempt from the sophisticated scammers after their initial 'Hi Son' scam failed to receive even one single reply.

EDUCATION

COUPLE DEMAND REFUND FROM PRIVATE SCHOOL AFTER CHILD FAILS TO TURN INTO ENTITLED PRICK

IN YET another sign that there are significant cracks in the foundations of Irish educational institutions, one local couple are exploring legal action after their son was moulded into a well-adjusted pupil disinclined to displays of arrogance and self-aggrandisement.

'We didn't pay €8,000 a year for my Milo to treat people well or have manners. You'll be hearing from my solicitors,' Jean and Greg Shields told the principal of St Deforus Preparatory School, one of the country's most prestigious and pompous secondary schools.

Apologising profusely for failing in their capacity as educators and moulders of men, teachers at the school insisted that it had never been their intention to have the 17-year-old pupil feel at ease with people from inferior economic backgrounds.

'He told us he hasn't pissed on one homeless person in all his years going to this school. I've no idea what you're teaching him, but it hasn't worked – he's never snapped his fingers in a restaurant and shouted "garçon",' raged Greg Shields, whose son now faces significant challenges in life.

'Milo's middle name is Tarquinius, for Christ's sake. You were supposed to be teaching him entitlement, and how he didn't have to put in any work because we'd bail him out every time.

He's put teaching – TEACHING – as his number one choice on the CAO,' added Jean.

The Shields were reassured that Milo's normal behaviour was 'just a phase' and that if they could get him into Smurfit Business School, a few years from now the damage should be reversed.

SOCIAL MEDIA

SOCIAL MEDIA

MAN SEEKS COURT INJUNCTION AGAINST EVER HAVING TO HEAR ABOUT BURKE FAMILY AGAIN

A MAN has been granted an injunction order against the Irish media, his WhatsApp groups, coworkers and social media networks, which prevents them from mentioning the Burke family to him ever again or they will face imprisonment for being in defiance of a court order.

Simon Clemons, 48, has had his fill of Burke-based news and, through his solicitors, he finally took the relevant action to make their existence an irrelevance to him.

'This injunction means that if I switch through radio stations in my car and so much as hear the beginnings of "Groundhog day again as noted eejit …" that radio station is off to jail,' confirmed Clemons outside the only court in Ireland a Burke probably wasn't within five metres of.

'So let it be known to my WhatsApp groups, that's an end to the memes; the only holy show I'll be watching this week is the papal funeral,' confirmed Clemons, who admitted he'd rather drag his testicles across

> **'So let it be known to my WhatsApp groups, that's an end to the memes'**

Council Notices

Dublin City Council defends decision to ban buskers from performing if they have fewer than five Grammy Awards.

a marathon course made entirely of cheese graters than have to hear about the Burke family again.

Clemons' legal representatives confirmed that if people wanted to discuss the Burke family disrupting the inquest into the death of a teenager or turning the WRC into a circus, there were plenty of people and media outlets willing to oblige.

'I don't care if he digs a tunnel from prison to the school while carrying a cross on his back, I'm not hearing any of it. I'm sick of it,' concluded Clemons.

𝔚aterford 𝔚hispers 𝔑ews

VOL 1, 26　　　　　　　WEDNESDAY 22 AUGUST 1922　　　　　　　2p

Sweet Suffering Jesus, Some Gowl Killed Collins

Some absolute gowl just shot Michael Collins in the head, *WWN* has learned. Seriously, some complete and utter gobshite murdered him in cold blood at Béal na Bláth during an ambush. Cork, what the fuck? Pure shame, like.

'Michael had a few pints with the lads in Long's Pub and when they headed home, some pack of hoors ambushed them and started shooting up the car,' one local man explained. 'Pure fucking gowls now the lot of them. Michael was pure sound, like, he started shooting back and all, but then he was sniped on the road and was dead before he hit the ground.'

It is understood Collins' body was brought back to Shanakiel Hospital in Cork, where it was confirmed he was 'dead as a doornail'.

'Oh, he's dead alright. Not a peep out of him. Sure look at him there, you'd expect him to sit up and start shouting Republican stuff,' a source at the small military hospital explained, as they prepared the body for burial. 'No point in doing an autopsy though. It's quite obvious by the gaping wound in his head that he died of that, ya know what I mean, boy?'

The ambush style sparked speculation that it was, in fact, the Anti-Treaty IRA who carried out the shooting, particularly a man named Sonny O'Neill.

'But who the hell knows really at this stage? Sure we've no detectives working for the guards yet as we're only a Free State a wet week,' another man rightly pointed out. Collins' final words were reportedly, 'Even revolutionaries need revenue and the confidence of the markets.'

Continued on Page 2

DRUG DEALER HAS DEBT WRITTEN OFF

A DUBLIN drug dealer who owed tens of thousands of euros for investments he made but lost to gardaí has had his debt written off, *WWN* has learned.

Tony Clear was estimated to owe over €90k for two kilos of cocaine he borrowed on the book from a local financial institution and drug cartel operating in the west Dublin region, but he ran into debt after gardaí discovered the stash in a nearby field, forcing him to appeal his case in the Street Courts.

A late-night hearing was called up the mountains and an agreement was made which granted Clear a full write-off in the guise of two nine-millimetre slugs behind his ear, one of dozens of such write-offs over the last 10 years.

'We're seeing a lot of dealers getting their debts written off this way,' one source explains. 'Obviously it's not fair on those who still owe large sums of money, but at least they're, you know, still alive.'

However, despite Clear being written off, his balance is expected to be passed on to his remaining family members.

THE ENVIRONMENT

HEADING TO THE BEACH AND COULDN'T GIVE A SHIT ABOUT RAW SEWAGE? HERE'S A MAP OF IRELAND'S RED FLAG BEACHES

ARE you and your family too hot to give a shite about swimming in hazardous materials? Why not try one of the dozens of suspiciously quiet beaches and waterways across the country that still allow millions of gallons of raw sewage to be discharged freely into the system?

With 43 areas where the Environmental Protection Agency (EPA) has stated that the rivers, lakes, estuaries and coastal waters are all contaminated with human and agricultural waste, there is no shortage of shit-soaked havens to let your family splash around and ingest all manner of highly dangerous parasites and organisms while cooling down in the hot summer sun.

Why not try Duncannon in the sunny southeast, where untreated water spews into the estuary daily? Or maybe Rush and Howth in Dublin, An Spideál and An Cheathrú Rua in

Things We've Learned as a Nation

Apartments in Bulgaria = good investment.

Galway, Kilmore Quay in Wexford? The list goes on, so you, too, can soak in some proper E. coli while developing serious health conditions.

Play 'toss the turd' in places like Merrion Strand or Youghal Front Strand. How about swallowing a nappy in Arklow or simply contracting an unknown virus in Ballycotton? The choices are endless.

Predictions for 2024

Micheál Martin will claim his go as Taoiseach didn't count as it was during lockdown, and wrestle back control.

PETS

'IT'S NOT THE DOG, IT'S THE OWNER' RULING SEES DOG OWNER PUT DOWN AFTER ATTACK

A HIGH Court ruling in a flagship case to euthanise a Dublin man instead of his dog after it attacked a pedestrian has been welcomed by animal lovers across the world.

'You shouldn't have been allowed own a budgie, never mind a Staffordshire Bull Terrier,' defendant Dermot Ryan was told by Judge Paul Riordan, after details emerged of how the 26-year-old would purposely antagonise the dog in a bid to 'make him look hard' while walking around the streets with his top off.

'My client is a skinny little runt who couldn't beat eggs with a sledgehammer and likes to act like he's the big man about town, so this was the obvious choice of dog for him to buy illegally from another insecure male friend,' defending barrister John Leemy pleaded with the Court.

The Court heard how Ryan 'sicked' his dog, Tyson, at a pedestrian who refused to give him the butt of their cigarette, before Tyson then bit her leg.

'She was horsing into a bleedin' Silk Cut 100, Judge. There was loads left on it and the mangey bitch told me to piss off, so Tyson got mad and nipped her leg – he was only protectin' me is all,' Ryan stated, before spitting onto the courtroom floor.

Considering the defendant's 467 previous convictions, Judge Riordan handed down the world's first ever death sentence for a dangerous dog breed owner, citing the fact, 'It's not the dog, it's the owner at fault here,'

before calling on the government and local councils to actually enforce laws that punish irresponsible idiots who own restricted breeds.

Ryan was later euthanised by a court-appointed vet.

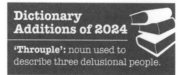

Dictionary Additions of 2024

'Throuple': noun used to describe three delusional people.

ROYALTY

HOW IRELAND IS CELEBRATING THE KING'S CORONATION

LIKE all other eight billion inhabitants of planet earth, the people of Ireland are 'Coronation Crazy' and the country is fit to burst with excitement at the prospect of King Charles donning a crown in front of an adoring and loyal public.

Here are all the ways Ireland is celebrating the historic occasion:

- Special masses will be laid on around Ireland, allowing people a place to pray for torrential rain to hit London.
- Getting the calculator out and working out how much good £100 million could do for poor people across Britain if it hadn't been spent on a party for Charles.
- Generally staring in the direction of England incredulously while wondering if they should contact NHS mental health professionals on England's behalf.
- Any horse born in Ireland on Coronation Day must bear the name Camilla.
- Invite Paul Burrell onto the *Late Late* to chat shit about Charles.
- Just like England came up with a 'coronation chicken' recipe in 1953 when Queen Elizabeth ascended the throne, Ireland has developed 'coronation manure', a signature manure which is made by combining the faeces of cows, sheep, pigs and other farm animals.
- A special line of King Charles tampons with his face on them are being sold in shops everywhere.
- Texting British friends with messages acknowledging this day of great significance for them, the texts largely pointing out the fact Charles won't be paying a penny of inheritance tax.

- Build Your Own Monarchy – one of the more fun events will see Irish people celebrate Charles by nominating their own 'royal family' in towns and villages. The rules are simple: find the most inbred person in your town, give them all the town's land for free and say 'Thank you' when they treat you with utter contempt.
- Cloning technology will allow The Wolfe Tones to play every pub in Ireland, meaning the nation can sing 'Celtic Symphony' in unison.

Council Notices

Due to a stagnation in funds, we have been forced to downgrade this year's Winter Wonderland to Winter Reduce Expectations Land.

UNESCO

SNOT ON PUB TOILET WALL GETS UNESCO WORLD HERITAGE STATUS

PROUDLY standing to the right of the now protected ball of mucus, publican John Shields smiled broadly as a member of UNESCO handed him a certificate guaranteeing recognition for the 15-year-old snot as a World Heritage site.

'If that snot could only talk,' Shields began, looking up at the long-crusted goo from an unknown source. 'The things it must have seen here in this toilet cubicle: the sex, the drugs, the rock and roll.'

Rumour has it the perfectly spherical ball of mucus originated at a trad session in 2008 and may have belonged to a famous Irish folk musician.

'I couldn't be telling now,' Shields went on, 'there was a lot of love put into that roll, with a flick to match. Whoever it was is a master of snot-rolling and should be proud today of this UNESCO World Heritage achievement.'

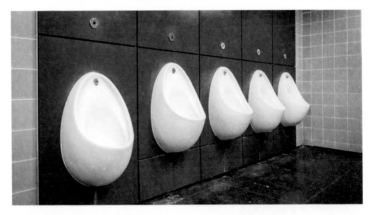

Now carefully laminated in a special varnish and encased in Perspex, the protected snot is expected to generate between €30–€40 for the local economy in the coming years through additional tourism.

BUSINESS PAGE OWNER UNDER IMPRESSION YOU WANT TO SEE PICTURES OF THEIR KIDS

HEALTH and fitness guru Lester Regan has somehow got the impression that his 1,276 Instagram followers want to suddenly see photographs of a family day out in a local park, *WWN* reports.

Showcasing the well-dressed kids in the public gallery, Regan posted the words, 'This is what it's all about,' followed by a lengthy space and several hundred hashtags pertaining to parenting and family.

'No one wants to see other people's kids, especially on a business page,' one former follower of Regan explained. 'I only followed him because his wife has a solid 10 arse – now that I've seen the kids, I can't help thinking how ruined she must be down there.'

Constantly refreshing his feed to view new interactions on the post, Regan's poor decision was encouraged by a cousin, who simply commented: 'dotes'.

'They're dressed like Mormons and look like they finally got a haircut,' Regan's friend Jonathan Reece points out. 'Those snotty-nosed little dirt magnets never look like that; they must have fostered the kids out for the day or something.'

Meanwhile, a study into business page etiquette has found that absolutely no one wants to see 'that bullshit' on their news feed, as the large majority of people can't stand other people's kids.

SOCIAL MEDIA

FIRE BRIGADE CALLED OVER TOXIC SPILLAGE FROM FAMILY WHATSAPP GROUP

WATERFORD emergency services were called this evening to a city centre home after a large toxic spillage was reported by a family member involved in a sibling WhatsApp group, *WWN* reports.

Quarantining the area, fire staff and paramedics tackled the oozing family group chat to no avail, as siblings squabbled and fought openly over various disagreements, leaving those trapped inside the group with serious third-degree burns and chronic anxiety issues.

'They just keep going back and the more they stay in there, the more toxic the so-called "family group" gets,' one paramedic said. 'Sisters undermining each other, brothers fighting over land, parents playing one set of siblings off another – it's the worst case we've dealt with in quite some time.'

Among the casualties were several teenage kids who were caught up in the blazing row and used as ammunition.

'We've tried to extinguish the initial he-said-she-said flare up, but once a family blaze like this is started there is only one outcome: a backdraft of vicious voice notes.'

Emergency services now fear the toxic spillage may seep into splinter groups of family members who have formed their own separate toxic WhatsApp groups.

TRAFFIC gardaí have taken to Twitter to post an image of a suspicious-looking Audi, which they pulled over after clocking the driver going 110 kmph in a 120 kmph zone.

'We also witnessed the car using indicators, so immediately our suspicions were flagged,' arresting Garda Gerry Moore said, explaining his reasoning.

It is understood the male driver in his late thirties was also very polite and courteous to gardaí when approached, raising concerns as to his motives.

'I asked the driver if he realised he's driving a brand new three-litre TDI, and he simply replied "yes",' Garda Moore recalls. 'At that moment I realised the man wasn't an Audi driver at all, and I tore him out of the driver's

GARDAÍ STOP SUSPICIOUS AUDI GOING UNDER THE SPEED LIMIT

seat and threw him to the ground before placing him in handcuffs.'

Following further investigation, gardaí found the driver to be registered to another, less expensive vehicle, and that he had borrowed the car from a friend to go on a Tinder date.

'Obviously he was trying to impress some quare one he met online and thought he could get away with passing himself off as an Audi driver,' Garda Moore added. 'Although he didn't break any laws *per se*, this form of catfishing is not acceptable, so I gave him a good boot up the hole before telling him to feck off back into the car, go home and cancel his date.'

The driver apologised to gardaí and promised to never drive an Audi like that ever again.

HEALTH

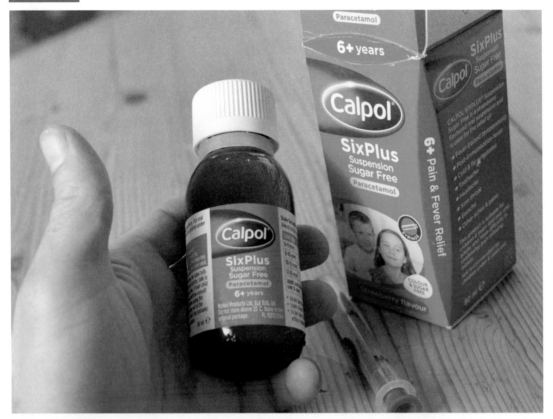

HOW THE CALPOL CRISIS DESTROYED NINETIES IRELAND

IF you enjoyed the TV show *Dopesick*, which documented the rise of the opioid crisis in America following the introduction of the painkilling drug oxycodone, then you should set your telly box to record the upcoming RTÉ drama *SickPlus*, which charts the devastating effects of Calpol on Irish society in the early 1990s.

For those too young to remember, the appearance of Calpol on the Irish market in the 1960s was a revolution for mothers (fathers in Ireland did not show an interest in their children before 2007). If your baby was crying due to a fever or toothache or tobacco withdrawals, you could simply give them a spoon of sweet-flavoured medicine without having to consult a local TD or the parish priest.

Flash forward 30 years to the early nineties, and you had grown-ups who were weaned on Calpol now having kids of their own. A generation who knew only one response to baby-related discomfort: reach for the Calpol.

It wasn't that Calpol didn't help to ease fevers and soothe pain, it was that parents around the country were dispensing it for every ailment the child had. Sore tummy? Calpol. Grazed arm? Calpol. Short sightedness? Calpol. As the TV show *SickPlus* documents, children were being treated for a range of fairly serious illnesses with just a strawberry-flavoured syrup.

In a further complication, the sweet taste of Calpol proved too much for even adults to resist.

Hundreds of parents were found to be unknowingly microdosing on Calpol due to their tendency to lick the spoon after distributing the medicine to their sick children.

It took almost 10 years and a multi-million-pound information campaign to teach parents that some illnesses are too severe for Calpol to treat, and that if their child presents symptoms such as a compound fracture, it would be best to take them to a medical professional instead of just 'doubling up the dose, just this once'.

Today, we know Calpol as the medicine that was supposed to be a sweet-tasting drop of paracetamol. But those of us who grew up in the nineties remember how bad it once was, when the 'pink opium' ran through society like a sticky river.

CRIME

SMALL-TOWN DRUG DETECTIVE HAS MAJOR LEAD ON LAD WHO USES WEED NOW AND AGAIN

ATTACHING clues to a large notice board with red wool thread he borrowed from his mother's house 10 years ago, local drug squad detective James Murray has what he believes is all the evidence he needs to apply for a warrant to search local cannabis user Colin Walsh's home.

'Uses cannabis: check. Knows other cannabis users: check. I just don't

like the cut of him: check,' Murray ticked off his checklist, before applying to the District Court to raid the family home of the 42-year-old man.

Despite the rural town being plagued with a series of unsolved crimes, Murray convinced Judge Stapleton to sign the warrant, pointing out that he had a reliable unnamed source confirming that Walsh did indeed use cannabis, and that Pulse showed he was caught in possession of a 10-spot 20 years ago.

'This is probably going to cause a huge vacuum in the local market,' Murray told fellow gardaí as they bashed down the door of the Walsh home, sparking untold irreversible

> **'This is probably going to cause a huge vacuum in the local market'**

anxiety in Walsh's young children.

'Bingo!' Murray confirmed as he found a tiny bit of weed in a sock, proving weeks of poor investigation, and potentially ruining the 'drug kingpin's' career, before illegally checking the target's smart phone and casually scrolling through intimate photographs with other non-detectives.

'Good job, ladies and gentlemen,' Murray exclaimed, acting like he just took down Pablo Escobar. 'Another few lives saved,' he added, before letting the suspect know he'll be seeing him again in three stressful years' time when the courts finally get around to it.

PETS

THIS DOG VISITS HIS OWNER'S GRAVE EVERY DAY TO SHIT ON IT

PREPARE to have your heart broken. Tissues at the ready because this is why we don't deserve dogs!

Chewie, an 11-year-old Yorkie, makes the three-kilometre journey from his deceased owner's home to his final resting place in a graveyard every day.

His owner, Trevor, passed away five months ago and, ever since then, Chewie hasn't failed to make the solo journey to the grave, where he does the most wretched-smelling, scuttery defecations one can imagine.

'Trevor was never one for giving out treats to the dog,' explained his widow and co-owner of Chewie, Barbara.

'Chewie was only delighted when Trevor croaked it. Trevor could get cranky and leave Chewie out in the garden if he barked too much, and Chewie never forgot it. He even tried to unplug the life support when he visited him in hospital,' explained Barbara.

The widow added that Chewie refrains from doing 'his business' until he has eaten breakfast and dinner, thus ensuring his graveyard visit will result in the largest possible deposit of vengeful shit.

'I wouldn't mind, but I've enough trouble cleaning up graffiti from teenagers, never mind arse graffiti,' explained the groundskeeper of the graveyard. 'I've never seen something so small deliver such large shits – the size of a baby's head the last one was. You can only produce that if you truly hate someone.'

NEARLY NOVEMBER AND LOCAL MAN STILL HASN'T LIT THE FIRE

ASTOUNDED he hasn't had to light the fire in his home so far this side of the new year, local man Karl Riordan has made it his business to let everyone know this trivial fact by crowbarring his unlit fire into every single conversation.

'Normally it would be roaring this time of year,' Riordan pointed out to his oblivious wife, his eyes manic with awe. 'October's almost gone now and there's not a speck of

ash in the fireplace, but she's ready to go whenever the air turns,' he added, looking out the window in anticipation.

Interestingly, Riordan famously highlighted the fact he had to light a fire on 5 June after an unusual cold snap, which saw temperatures fall to six degrees.

'Mad, isn't it? You could be lighting a full-blown fire in June and then not even so much as a fire log in October,' he continued with his riveting observation, now to a work colleague who also wasn't paying much attention. 'I did light a few candles the other night just to give the sitting room a nice warm glow for ambience, but we're nowhere near buying a bag of coal and some wooden logs yet.'

Taking to social media in the hopes of sparking praise for his incredible observation, Riordan snapped a picture of a lone candle placed neatly in his empty fireplace with the caption, 'I hope the weather stays like this for the whole winter lol,' which received zero interactions or likes.

'Facebook's gone to shite lately, no one on the fecking thing anymore,' he told himself, before turning on the radiators for an hour in pure disgust.

EXCLUSIVE

MAN HAS WAITED YEARS FOR CHANCE TO MOON GOOGLE STREETVIEW CAR

BY day Waterford man Liam Parsons stands at his curtains watching, and by night he searches online for scheduling clues, all in the hopes that one day he will be there when the Google Streetview car drives past his home so he can enter internet history forever.

'The last appearance in this area was 2011, so we're due an update,' said Parsons.

'I haven't decided what I want to do yet – if you do something too graphic like hang your balls out of your trousers, the Google car's built-in ball-blurring technology will just erase you. It's mad that someone had to sit down and develop testicle-blurring technology. But anyways, I think I can get away with flashing my brown, hairy arse out of the top window. That's my aim, that's my goal.'

Committing oneself to visual history by gesturing at a passing camera-equipped vehicle is nothing new, with Parsons himself admitting that he still owns the aerial portrait of his family home that was done by helicopter in the 1980s, where as a boy he can be clearly seen giving it a two-finger salute from the front garden.

'My dad would always look at that picture and say, "Liam, don't be a bollox all your life",' said Parsons, 45, destined to prove him wrong.

> **'I think I can get away with flashing my brown, hairy arse out of the top window.'**

TRANSPORT

GALWAY GIVEN LUAS FOR ONE-WEEK TRIAL

CHOKED BY traffic and awaiting a €600 million ring road, Galway is to be given the Luas for an exclusive one-week trial to see if frequent public transport with the capacity to carry hundreds of passengers is something they would like full time.

'What the fuck was that?' said one motorist, swerving out of the way

> **'I've missed all my children's major life milestones due to being stuck in traffic'**

of a bell-ringing Luas heading in the NUIG direction.

To ensure Galway gets to experience the true Luas journey, the trams will come preinstalled with trouble-making teens and pricks playing music from their phones at full blast.

'You know I could get used to this,' said one of the first Galway Luas passengers as they breezed past idle cars on Headford Road and Quincentennial Bridge. 'I've missed all my children's major life milestones due to being stuck in traffic, but this changes everything.'

However, the trial ran into some problems when motorists in Salthill blocked the passage of one Luas.

'It's bad enough with cyclists, but I hate nothing more than people getting places quicker than me and without the blood-pressure-rising stress I endure in the car,' said one motorist, now lying across the ground in protest.

At the end of the trial, locals will be asked to fill in a comment card with their feedback, and if most people want a light rail system introduced to Galway, the government has pledged to get back to them with plans in 2060.

CRIME

THE ELIMINATOR: HERE'S WHAT WE KNOW ABOUT THE MONK'S LETHAL HEAD OF SECURITY

WITH THE Monk attracting a media frenzy after being found not guilty of the murder of David Byrne, *Whispers World* investigates Hutch's inner circle and the mysterious protector we can only speculate is his head of security, whom we've now coined 'The Eliminator' in a bid to further increase sales of our Sunday edition.

Basing all our intel on third-party information and blatant hearsay from sources who may or may not be telling the truth, which won't stop us anyway, we detail the life and crimes of gangland Ireland's most trusted henchman.

'I know him, yeah, he once took out an entire block of flats because someone robbed The Monk's second cousin's budgie,' said one source, who conveniently for us wants to remain anonymous. 'He entered the flats at 9 a.m. and by 9.05 a.m. everyone was dead in a large pile outside.'

'Heard he secretly took out the Queen last year 'cause Gerry owed the IRA a favour,' explains another reliable source we can't name in case someone actually researches the claim. 'Sneaked into the palace one night when she was asleep and shoved his hand down her throat and squeezed her heart like a plum – security were too ashamed to admit it, though.'

Singlehandedly managing The Monk's exit from the Special Criminal Court yesterday afternoon, it was no wonder The Monk looked confident of his safety, not even arranging a lift home for himself.

'The Eliminator issued a gangland curfew for the entire city yesterday,' another source we may have made up this time said. 'Kinahans know better than to even dare make a move, as he would have Dubai blitzed in a heartbeat, Arabs and all.'

The Eliminator, who fended off press outside the court, was heard muttering the words, 'Yer animals, leave him grieve in peace,' a code we are told means, 'I'll have your entire families, even your pets dismembered with a rusty hacksaw blade duct taped to a melted toothbrush.'

Read more about The Eliminator in our 4,567-page special in this week's *Whispers World*, or listen to our 10-hour podcast special sponsored by some dodgy online gambling site that's secretly run by the Russian mafia.

BREAKING

SCHOOL MOVES OVERNIGHT TO AVOID ENOCH BURKE

THINGS HAVE gone from bad to worse for Enoch Burke as, in addition to news that he will be fined €700 for each day he attends Wilson's Hospital School, the injunction-ignorer arrived at the property this morning to find it was moved to a secret location overnight.

Small, subtle remnants of the school remain in place, such as a discarded pencil here and there, but Burke, who had planned a day of lingering at the gates, was shocked to discover his former employer had finally had enough.

'The process wasn't easy, it had to be done brick by brick and reassembled here at our new anonymous location, but you'd be surprised at the number of volunteers willing to help kids learn in fucking peace without the nation's media

Things We've Learned as a Nation

Speaking on your phone while driving is apparently still illegal, even if you're holding your phone like a little plate and talking into the bottom of it.

outside the front door every day,' confirmed the school's groundskeeper.

The school, formerly of Multyfarnham, Westmeath, came up with the novel solution to a former employee turning up uninvited every day after a brainstorming session.

'We've sort of placed ourselves in the At-Our-Wits-End Protection Programme, and here we can just get on with things. It's great,' admitted staff and pupils at the school.

Quotes of The Year

'Could you please explain the words "State", "built", "social" and "housing" to me one more time?'
– **Darragh O'Brien**

While the school's location will not be disclosed, it is rumoured to be on a large, steep hill with a crocodile-filled moat at its base.

THE ENVIRONMENT

BLUE LOBSTER JUST DEPRESSED

A RARE blue lobster caught in Belfast Lough by a County Down fisherman has bravely opened up about its mental health struggles in a tell-all interview with *WWN*, stating its life is not all the glitz and glamour the media perceives it to be.

Labelled as a 'one in two million find', Lazerian the Lobster thanked the local and national newspapers for the publicity, but said it wanted to use its 15 minutes of fame to highlight the issues blue lobsters go through daily.

'The name-calling from other lobsters like "willow pattern head" and "fancy clamps" doesn't faze me, but it's the sheer loneliness of being such a rare breed that gets me down,' Lazerian revealed, who admits to a

love of listening to Damien Dempsey. 'People think you're special but try living in Belfast being the odd one out – up here you're either one side or another, but if you're neither it's tough going.'

Begging for the fisherman not to throw him back in, Lazerian said he yearned for a nice boiling pot of salted water, and only for his weight he'd be on a plate in some fancy Michelin-starred restaurant right now, sliding down a wealthy oesophagus.

'Lovely gesture throwing me back in and all, but I was kind of hoping to be lathered in garlic butter and cracked open like an egg,' he added. 'A knife through my cranium or just a good old-fashioned boiling alive would

have sufficed, but no, Mister Goody-two-shoes fucked me back in with this miserable bunch of racist crustaceans – cheers for that.'

LINGUISTS around the world have admitted that they're 'stumped' when it comes to understanding how people from Northern Ireland have managed to form a language consisting of nothing more than high-pitched whines and snorts, *WWN* can report.

'There are chimpanzee communities in the deepest jungles of the world that can communicate using 13 to 14 basic throat sounds. Nordies have it down to three,' said Dr Kellen Muster, author of *Northern Man and the Quest for Understanding*, published today.

'I myself spent weeks living in Northern Ireland as an observer to see how they have bridged the gap from noise to language. I've drunk Harp with these people. Marched with these people. And through it all, I've remained astounded by their ability to understand each other, even when nobody else can.'

Although Dr Muster laughed off any suggestion that we may one day be able to hold a conversation with a person who lives north of Newry, he did state that people should not let

CRAZY HOW NORDIES CAN UNDERSTAND EACH OTHER

the lack of communication tools stop them from visiting Northern Ireland.

'In stores and pubs, simply point and make a noise that sounds like "at-dur". That should work on most

people. "At dur!" you'll say, and they'll give you a bottle of Buckfast or fireworks or a big box of Daz or whatever it is you're pointing at,' he told us.

BREAKING ▬▬▬▬▬▬

MAN'S CAUSE OF DEATH LISTED AS 'WAITING LIST'

A 55-YEAR-OLD man has had his cause of death listed as 'waiting list' by a coroner, *Waterford Whispers News* can confirm.

One of many Irish people on a lengthy waiting list before the pandemic, which exacerbated the problem, Dermot Grafton was in line for an endoscopic surgery – an investigative procedure to identify the cause of a stomach problem – but a shortage of beds, staff and fucks given by the State meant the procedure never took place.

Idiotically thinking that, due to living in a country which proclaims it has a public health service model, he didn't need private health insurance, Grafton died after his stomach

ruptured and an ambulance took over an hour to reach his home.

'It was the perfect storm of waiting list and ambulance shortage, but thankfully this is the first such recorded case ever in Ireland so others can take some solace in that,' said the coroner during the inquest.

'True, the acute gastric dilation he experienced was fatal, but it's the waiting list that did it,' added the coroner.

Experts in the Irish health game have expressed little sympathy for Grafton, who leaves behind a wife and four children.

'Every fool knows that you don't just accept at face value that you're on a waiting list and will be called.

You've got to quit your job and dedicate all your time and patience to ringing your GP's receptionist, the consultant's receptionist, your local TD, the hospital, then start a campaign, organise a protest, get private health insurance – duh! – go on Joe Duffy, and go through this cycle six or seven times before you can get seen to,' explained one expert, annoyed that someone could complain about such a system.

MIDDLE-CLASS COUPLE WORRIED THEY MIGHT HAVE TO PROTEST LIKE WORKING-CLASS SCUM

A DUBLIN couple struggling to maintain their rent, pay bills and get on the housing ladder, despite being on a reasonably good income, fear they may yet have to protest like the working-class scum they constantly see being put down on the news.

'Ever since the lunatics highjacked the water meter protests a few years ago, taking to the street and voicing your concerns just doesn't have that same *je ne sais quoi* anymore,' said Jack Freeman, explaining his predicament. 'We don't want to be lumped in with those feral clowns out every weekday stopping traffic because they've been duped into hating refugees, egged on by racist lads' non-stop tweeting from home. We shop in BTs for Christ's sake, my parents have an AGA in their kitchen!'

Echoing her partner's sentiments, Laura Ryan called for some distinction to be made between looney protests, fuelled by misinformation the government seems only too happy to allow fester, and legitimate protests like ones they didn't attend during the abortion referendum but did 'like' on social media.

'Protests give me the ick. I used to think they were beneath me but

if Leo (big fan, don't get the hate) and the guys continue gaslighting us on the housing crisis, I might have to protest what's going on in this country, but only as long as no one I know sees me on the

telly. I don't want to look like an absolute raving mad cunt, protesting a factory shutting or something,' the accountant added, her head now firmly in her hands with bills scattered across the kitchen table.

TRANSPORT

DUBLIN BUS UNVEILS FIRST MONSTER BUS

SWIFTLY responding to a video circulating of one of their buses mounting a path to avoid traffic congestion, Dublin Bus has confirmed a new addition to its fleet.

'It's on a trial basis for now but if it's successful we'll convert the whole fleet,' said a Dublin Bus spokesperson unveiling a number 16 monster-truck bus with 1,500 horsepower.

'Chockablock during the school run? No problem, this lad will easily navigate through traffic and save journey time by flattening the fuck out

> **'This lad will easily navigate through traffic and save journey time by flattening the fuck out of everything in its path'**

of everything in its path,' explained the spokesperson, who was barely audible during a test run in Terenure, such was the volume of screams from motorists.

The innovation in public transport will require passengers to initially scale the 12-foot distance up to the bus doors, but plans are underway to convert some of the stops to be fitted with trampolines to make it easier.

Reacting to claims that a fleet of monster trucks will crush motorists to death as they sit in their cars, the Dublin Bus spokesperson grew visibly frustrated.

'Jesus, we can't win with you people: "Oh, the bus is never on time", "Where's the bus?", "That bus mounted the path to get to the next stop quicker, it's a disgrace", "The monster truck flattened my granny". Honestly, can you hear yourselves?'

RELATIONSHIPS

MAN WISHES HE WAS SINGLE AGAIN SO HE CAN HOOK UP WITH ZERO WOMEN LIKE HE USED TO

'WHERE were all these young ones in my day?' 37-year-old Vincent Potts asked himself, suffering a severe case of 'missing out' as he drove his wife and two young children through a busy seaside town on a hot summer's afternoon, wondering where it all went right.

Adjusting his jet-black Ray Bans in case his eye direction was noticed by his wife of six years, Potts yearned for his youth again – a time when he used to go out with his mates four times a week and hook up with zero women.

> **'It would be totally different now as I'm way more confident in myself'**

'No, it would be totally different now as I'm way more confident in myself,' the 19-stone factory worker insisted, copperfastening all his logic in favour of fantasy, building himself up for a sneaky wank in the shower later when he finally gets some alone time.

'Jaysis, she'd want to put some clothes on her or she'll catch her death,' Potts blurted, after realising his wife caught him staring at what he hoped was a legal-aged woman wearing a bikini.

'Fuck sake, Vinny, get it together, man. She's on her flowers now and she'll be in a mood for the week if you're not careful,' his head echoed, wishing back his youth when he had no money, career, life goals, girlfriend, and wanked into a sock several times a day because he was usually too stoned to chat to members of the opposite sex.

CRIME

KINAHANS CONSIDERING COMING HOME AFTER SEEING MESS POLICE MADE OF HUTCH CASE

RUMOURS have been circulating since late yesterday evening that members of the Kinahan family are seriously considering returning home, feeling whatever arrests and charges they would be subjected to are no match for the DPP and the guard's ability to snatch defeat from the jaws of victory.

'I do miss an auld 99 back home, haven't had a decent chipper in ages, and what's the worst that could happen? A few weeks in the dock before some judges absolutely roast the State's star witness for having a story with more holes in it than a Swiss cheese factory. Be grand,' confirmed one Kinahan, already booking a flight home.

Already growing out their beards and hair, the Kinahans are said to be looking forward to placing their

feet on Irish soil once more to face a prosecution case put together by a bunch of transition year students on work experience.

'Handcuffs made of jelly, I'd rather take my chances with the DPP than get collared by the FBI on me holliers

here in Dubai,' added another, who was reassured by his legal team that even if the DPP had him banged to rights on unpaid parking tickets, they would inexplicably instead charge him with planning 9/11.

'There was us actually shitting ourselves, and for what? If the Irish State fell into a barrel of tits it'd come up sucking its thumb.'

In response through a joint statement, the guards and the DPP admitted that despite watching *The Usual Suspects* for a fortieth time, they still have no idea as to who Keyser Söze is.

LOCAL MAN UNAWARE HE'S SHARING DAD MEMES

WATERFORD man and self-confessed 'legend' Darren Roche is seemingly unaware that he has somehow transitioned into a lame meme-sharing dad, *WWN* has learned.

'It all started when he posted one of those old newspaper cartoons depicting a chair-bound, TV-watching husband with his wife pottering around, and a crudely altered caption that I didn't bother reading,' former friend of Roche, Hayden Leemy recalled, who now uses past tense when talking about Roche like he's

dead. 'We first put it down as a slip up, but then the "I identify" memes began and it just started escalating from there.'

Presumably while wearing brown tartan slippers with a blanket over his legs, 37-year-old Roche continually bombarded his feed with pixelated screengrabs he copied and pasted from 'funny' meme groups he joined, flooding friends' timelines and WhatsApp groups like he was on a mission to destroy comedy for good.

'I unfollowed him after he started his Dilbert phase,' wife Clarinda Roche confirmed. 'When the anti-Meta rants began, calling everyone online "woke" and saying no one has a sense of humour anymore, I served

him with divorce papers, which is when the ex-wife memes began.'

Now only speaking in dated memes, Roche defended his hobby with the classic sarcastic smiling Willy Wonka meme with the quote "It's not that I'm not listening, it's just that I don't care", followed by a Barack Obama mic-drop GIF for good measure.

DRINKING

'MAY MAKE PEOPLE LOOK MORE ATTRACTIVE THAN THEY ACTUALLY ARE': NEW ALCOHOL WARNINGS REVEALED

NEW regulations that will require all alcohol to carry warning labels have been signed into law by Minister for Health Stephen Donnelly today. The regulations will see the following health warnings attached to all alcohol products going forward:

- 'Any more than two beers can render people over thirty hungover for an entire week'
- 'May make people look more attractive than they actually are'
- 'Will give terrible singers the false impression they can sing'
- 'Nothing added but time … in prison'

- 'Known to increase cases of "what the fuck are you lookin' at, y'cunt?"'
- 'Buckfast makes you fuck fast'
- 'Will break the seal after three drinks and leave you pissing for the night'
- 'May encourage dancing to "Rock the Boat" at weddings'
- 'Promotes memory loss of embarrassing moments, including hit and runs and assaults'
- 'Will make you promise to meet people the next day when you least want to meet people'
- 'Grand with antibiotics'
- 'May make men look pregnant'

- 'This wine is not to be drunk like beer, you absolute fucking savage'
- 'Just because Jesus drank it, it doesn't mean you can pour wine on your cereal every morning, Tina!'
- 'High risk of pissing in wardrobe'
- 'There's easier and cheaper ways to alienate yourself from family and friends'
- 'Carries increased risk of being star of tomorrow's viral video entitled "crazy racist goes on rant at takeaway staff"'
- 'Worked wonders for George Best'
- 'First sip may encourage phone calls to local coke dealers'

EXCLUSIVE

MAN KICKING HIMSELF FOR SAYING SORRY TO STRANGER WHO GOT IN HIS WAY

KICKING himself for what must be the ten thousandth time in his lifetime, Conor Maher vowed to never apologise for anything ever again after a man barged towards him out of a shop entrance, forcing him to step back out of his way while somehow saying sorry.

'Why did I say sorry? He's the bollocks storming out and getting in my way,' Maher chastised himself, sickened he didn't 'clothesline the cunt' instead and then dance on his head. 'He didn't even have the decency to acknowledge my saying

sorry, just brushed past me like I was toenail dirt.'

Maher's track record for saying sorry for things he didn't do is believed to have stemmed from his polite upbringing in rural Ireland, where everyone says sorry for things that carry no fault.

'This is mostly a culchie-based phenomenon where the culchie believes deep down that their entire existence is the problem,' believes apology expert Dr David Stapleton. 'Rural folk say sorry on average 500 times per day for things that carry no

real blame, like getting in someone's way, but they are unable to process the encounter without apologising for simply being there. We found that if a culchie could just disappear forever at these moments, they would.'

Conor Maher has since taken a new approach for such an encounter.

'Now, instead of saying sorry, I just tell people to get the fuck out of my way,' he informed us. 'I find this is a lot more enjoyable and people seem to respect me more for the honesty.'

Quotes of The Year

'They let me wear the big boy hat and everyone clapped, and those who didn't were arrested by the Met.'
- King Charles

BREAKING

NATION'S LAST AVAILABLE PLUMBER DIES

THERE was bad news on the home improvements front today as the last plumbing contractor in Ireland with any availability this side of Christmas passed away following a short illness, leaving thousands of homes with no chance of getting a few jobs done around the house.

'The death has occurred of Peter Hanlon, 55, peacefully in his residence

surrounded by phones ringing out,' read the late plumber's RIP.ie page.

'The Hanlon family would like to extend our condolences to anyone who Peter had in his book for jobs over the next few months, from the downstairs bathroom conversion jobs to the radiators that aren't heating up, which you could probably fix yourself with a vent key and a YouTube tutorial,' added the online obituary.

'Peter was a rare one: a plumber who would actually answer his phone when you rang him,' confirmed one Dublin man, robbed of getting a leaky tap fixed before it rolled into its second year of drippiness.

'What am I supposed to do now, rely on my idiot brother-in-law who owns two spanners and thinks he's Tim Allen from *Home Improvement*?' wailed another woman we spoke to, while wandering the streets waving fistfuls of cash at any white van that drove past with a length of copper on its roof rack.

WWN would like to pass on its condolences to Mr Hanlon's family and kindly ask for any available plumbers still alive out there to please leave their name in the comments – the toilet has been clogged for months and we can't live like this anymore.

45-YEAR-OLD STILL RINGS TO LET EVERYONE KNOW HE GOT HOME SAFE

WHAT is the cut-off age for giving people a 'quick jingle' to let them know you're home safe? That's the question being asked by 45-year-old midlands man Eamon O'Malley, who to this day cannot enter the front door of his house without letting the last person he saw know that he's still in one piece.

'Eamon, we're in our forties, we're grown men. You don't need to send me a "safe and sound" text, really,' said one of O'Malley's pals, who has tolerated this behaviour for decades.

'I know it's recommended to women to do things like this, but dude, we're men. We're not at that high of a risk of

not making it home safely. Your pals are not sitting around worried about who may or may not have followed you up the road. It's one of the perks of being a man, so y'know, enjoy it. Quit sending me voicemails at two in the morning, please.'

Nevertheless, O'Malley has resolved to continue sending the irritating-but-reassuring texts to whomever he spoke to last on a night out, despite nobody ever letting him know if they got home alive or not.

'How hard is it to text "Hey, had a nice time, home safe and sound, talk to you later"?' Anyways, nice talking to you, just arrived at the house there, let

me know if you need anything else,' said O'Malley in a text to us, an hour after we wrapped up our interview with him.

ARCHITECTURE

THE SPIRE 20 YEARS ON: DUBLINERS SHARE THEIR THOUGHTS

Council Notices

Waterford Council apologises for our decision to install dangerous mood swings in a number of playgrounds.

CELEBRATING its 20th birthday dominating Dublin's skyline, the divisive figure of The Spire splits opinion to this day, but 20 years on, what do locals make of it?

'I suppose it's a handy landmark for tourists wondering which part of the city they should avoid'
– **David, 39**

'I like to stick fridge magnets to it'
– **Maureen, 59**

'One second I'm scribbling trying to get my pen to work, next thing I know that scribble was accepted as the design for The Spire by Dublin City Council'
– **Ian Ritchie, architect, 79**

'I usually piss on it for good luck'
– **Noel, 44**

'You know something has truly been accepted by the local people when it has a nickname, for example, I call it "that fucking eyesore"'
– **Aiden, 28**

'I think the only thing it has going for it is that if they tried to build it today, it'd have somehow cost €4 billion, not €4 million'
– **Sinead, 33**

'You could build a second spire with the number of discarded syringes on O'Connell Street'
– **Cian, 67**

'Like, what's it even pointing at?'
– **Declan, 34**

'They say it even took the Parisians a while to come around to the Eiffel Tower, but at least you can climb up that fucking yoke'
– **Aleksander, 48**

'Mad to think aliens built it'
– **Caitríona, 22**

'I like the way it does fuck all'
– **Peter, 51**

'The Spire is a unique tourist attraction, insofar as not a single tourist is attracted to it'
– **Sarah, 47**

'I can't believe it wasn't a joke. I remember when I first saw it, I thought "Holy shit, they were actually serious?!"'
– **remaining population of Dublin**

Predictions for 2024

Vladimir Putin's three-day, easypeasy conquering of Ukraine will incur yet more unforeseen delays.

FINANCE

US DEBT HITS $40 TRILLION AFTER BIDEN BUYS ROUND IN TEMPLE BAR

THE US economy is teetering on the brink of imminent collapse after president Joe Biden unwisely offered to buy a round in a Temple Bar pub during his visit to Dublin.

'The wallet was out and he was all, "Let's stick this on the business credit card." It was over before I could

stop him,' said one aide, recalling the moment Biden bought eight pints of Guinness, pushing the US total debt from the reasonable $32 trillion mark to an unmanageable $40 trillion.

Stock markets tanked at the news that Biden had exercised poor financial judgement by believing that buying a few pints in a

> **'The wallet was out and he was all, "Let's stick this on the business credit card"'**

Dublin tourist hot spot would cost less than a war in the Middle East.

'I think we could have ridden this one out, maybe called in the IMF to take on a small fraction of the Temple Bar bill debt, but then Joe bought the packet of Tayto,' said one despairing aide.

The Tayto, a single packet of the Irish snack staple, which was to be shared among the eight people hovering around a crowded table in the pub, somehow cost €3.95, tipping the scales on the US national debt.

'The world's economy is in freefall, we repeat, freefall. This will forever be known as the Temple Bar Depression,' said news anchors reporting on the incident, not even referring to the mental state of the person forced to wear the leprechaun costume around Temple Bar.

WW news

Waterford Whispers News

WORLD NEWS

'WE WON'T HAVE TRUE EQUALITY UNTIL THEY'RE NAMED THE HERMALAYAS'

A GROUP of feminists, who insist they aren't just a men's rights group trying to drum up a stupid story that the media will run without any additional research, have said it is high time the highest peaks of the world are recognised by their true gender.

'Do you want an actual quote to go with this pile of utter brain wank that no one in their right mind should believe but will anyway? Or do you think the headline will be enough for it to become one of the most talked about news stories in the world this week, ahead of violence against women, the murder of trans people, child exploitation, etc?' queried feminist group HerMountainToClimb.

'This is a genuine claim and news story which proves your deeply held view that the world has gone mad and that you'd be put in jail for saying "Himalayas" now,' said HMTC before adding that Greta Thunberg supports the cause if that'll boil your piss.

'Silly stuff like this is definitely at the summit of feminists' concerns, please take this at face value,' concluded HMTC.

Elsewhere, opinion columnists have delighted in the news, stating, 'That's this week's arse vomit of a column sorted so,' before doing no further research and fist pumping the air after realising there's some clever wordplay to be done around 'sHERpa'.

LAID-OFF TECH WORKER ALWAYS FEARED THE DAY WOULD COME WHEN HE'D HAVE TO DO REAL WORK

THE announcement of more job losses at PayPal and Google has resulted in many tech workers realising that their parents were right all along: 'computers' wasn't a 'real job' and they should have taken up a trade like their cousin.

'You know, for a minute there I really believed that I could make a long and fruitful career for myself in an industry where I could put both my skills and my interests to good use, but it turns out I should have just listened to dad and gotten a job in the civil

service. A job for life, as he put it,' said one software engineer we spoke to.

'There's about to be tens of thousands of us laid off around the world by the biggest companies like Meta and Microsoft and the like, so it's going to be very hard to find work in my chosen field. It goes to show, listen to your parents when they tell you which dreams to follow, they know best.'

Meanwhile, a think-tank of dads operating out of a Waterford pub have crowed about how they 'saw all this coming' and expressed hope that young people would finally catch a hold of themselves.

'Youngsters planning their lives aren't going to want to hear this, but not everyone can have a nice cushy soft-hands job with a ping pong table and a subsidised canteen,' said one dad we spoke to, who was finding it hard to hide his glee that nobody was going to have an easier life than the one he found himself slogging through.

Elsewhere, career guidance teachers are being advised not to recommend jobs in the tech industry to students who display an aptitude for mathematics, computer science or creativity, and instead point them towards something more recession-proof like construction or hospitality.

Quotes of The Year 66

'It's hard not to laugh at how all of this has turned out.'
- Bernie Sanders

GUN CRIME

'THAT MASS SHOOTING IN AMERICA IS AWFUL,' SAYS WOMAN WHO IS GOING TO HAVE TO BE MORE SPECIFIC

SUCH is the horrifying frequency of mass shootings in America, local woman Andrea O'Reardon is going to have to be more specific when conveying her utter devastation to her work colleagues about yet more needless loss of life.

'Is it the hate-crime shooting where trans and gay people were gunned down in a gay club? The one where hateful right-wing talking heads on social media and Fox News are practically celebrating, that one? Or the Walmart one?' asked one of O'Reardon's colleagues, who was wincing and bracing themselves for news of a different, even more recent shooting.

With over 700 mass shootings in the US in 2022, there has been an increase in confusion and crossed wires when people seek to share their sincere anger and desolation over another shooting, which seems to have little effect on Republican politicians' willingness to introduce safer gun laws.

'Oh my God, I just saw that on the news, so, so awful. I honestly can't comprehend how mundane yet tragic they feel to some people over there. Wait, Andrea, are you talking about the ones in Philadelphia and Maryland yesterday or the Walmart in Virginia the day before, or the ones in Florida or Oklahoma on the same day? There was a racially motivated one and another homophobic one, was it them?' inquired another coworker who wandered into the reception area.

Now unsure if she had the correct and specific details on which

Predictions for 2024

Fresh out of original ideas, God announces Covid 24.1.

incident made her stomach sink as if weighed down by a dozen anchors, O'Reardon opened up Google on her phone to clarify which bullet-strewn crime scene that had robbed people of their loved ones and made yet more orphans, widows and widowers brought her to the verge of tears.

'You know what, just gimme a minute, it's saying here there's been 5,000 mass shootings over there in less than a decade … it's going to take me a little time to find the one I'm talking about,' sighed O'Reardon.

CRIME

WHAT SENTENCES WOULD THESE NOTORIOUS CRIMINALS GET IN IRISH COURTS TODAY?

AT TIMES accused of maddening and incomprehensible leniency that offends victims of crimes, the Irish judiciary is coming in for renewed criticism after a series of cases involving suspended sentences for grievous crimes.

WWN, wanting to show that such frustrations are the fault of the stupid public who have no appreciation for the vagaries of the law, presented a number of Irish judges with the outlines of cases involving the world's most notorious criminals (names redacted) and asked them what punishment, if any, they would garner were they to come before the courts.

Pol Pot
'Who among us hasn't every now and again fallen prey to our own ill temper? Would we not be the kettle to Mr Pot if we were to impose a prison sentence? Mr Pot, it is a suspended sentence I shall give to you today. But don't think of it suspended over you like the sword of Damocles – just go out and enjoy your life, have a bit of craic.'

Ted Bundy
'I appreciate the suffering the victims and their families have been put through, but at the end of the day he has a character reference from a local priest, so …'

Charles Ponzi
'We must retain a sense of perspective in a world which seeks to distort it. Mr Ponzi is not a good-for-nothing cannabis smoker, he is an honest businessman who let his love of pyramids unduly influence his conduct. I would consider it an honour to invest in whichever business venture he chooses to start when I let him free from this court in a moment.'

Bonnie and Clyde
'The purpose of this court is not to provide an "eye for an eye" style of mob justice. I am assured by the accused, and I am inclined to believe their contrition when they say they got an awful fright firing those guns and robbing those banks, and that the tears of those they were tormenting were quite upsetting to witness. Lesson learned.'

Fred and Rose West
'Why this case has even passed the threshold for prosecution and come before the Court in the first place is a mystery; this is a matter for Tusla.'

Mark 'Chopper' Read
'With a considerable number of previous convictions, I have no option but to declare you a scamp and a rapscallion. Now off home with you!'

Your mate who smoked a spliff last year
'A custodial sentence is the regrettable justice I choose as a warning to others. In addition to the 20-year sentence, once released the plaintive is not permitted within five miles of a plant of any description, cannabinoid in nature or not.'

Harold Shipman
'To come into court and impugn the reputation of someone who, I would surmise, could be a fellow member of my golf club is unconscionable. Truly *malum impunis in extremis*. And while it is not in my power to direct the jury to call for a defunct punishment such as the death penalty, I would be tempted to do so, but for the accusers in this case.'

Jeffrey Epstein
'These alleged crimes are admittedly on the lower end of the scale of sexual crimes and surely being brought before the Court is punishment and shame enough.'

RELIGION

POPE USES EASTER SUNDAY MASS TO CRITICISE SHRINKING SIZE OF EASTER EGGS

POPE FRANCIS, the leader of the Catholic Church, has made an unprecedented intervention during his annual celebration of Easter Sunday mass to rage against the shrinking size of Easter eggs.

'And don't get me started on the fucking bars, those thieving-prick

Bill's Political Tips

Bookmark RIP.ie and visit any wakes in your area. Every day, go to another wake, shake some hands and get some goodwill ... and mileage expenses.

chocolate companies try to palm you off with two mini bars,' the Pope said from the pulpit, in front of a large congregation of worshipers.

'In my day, you used to get two bars minimum with an egg – be fucking lucky to get the one these days. Tight gits,' added the Pope before displaying a series of eggs on the altar from previous Easters, which charted the very visible reduction in size of chocolate eggs.

Dancing around making a direct and explicit threat to Cadbury executives, the Pope said he would empathise with Catholics who resorted to violence over the issue, and he

would find it very easy to forgive them during confession.

'And don't fall for forking out 40 blips for a big, fancy, "luxury" chocolate egg. Taste like fecking cardboard them ones do,' cautioned the Pope, ruminating on this year's Mass theme of 'Easter has gone to the dogs altogether'.

The Pope was then forced to deny an accusation made by one parishioner of a similar reduction in the portion size of communion wafers.

BETTER NAME NEEDED FOR THIS STUFF

'ABSOLUTELY fucking anything else' has topped a recent poll asking the public what would be a better name for the yellow-bloomed, oil-producing plant currently known as 'rapeseed', *WWN* can report.

Rapeseed, sometimes shortened to 'rape', is commonly farmed for the production of rape oil in large fields of rape, none of which sits well with 99.99% of the population, who have asked that a better name be sourced for the whole thing.

'We appreciate that the name of the plant is derived from the Latin word "*rapum*", meaning "turnip", and apparently they're all part of the same family – that's all understandable, no issues there. But it also shares its name with, y'know, "rape",' said a member of the Rapeseed Renaming Committee.

'In all honesty, it wouldn't matter what the etymology of it was; if potatoes were called "haemorrhoids", we'd have renamed them decades ago. The population has had enough of feeling icky every time they buy a bottle of rapeseed, or when their

kids ask, 'Hey, what do you call that stuff growing in those big yellow fields over there?' Call the stuff "yellowflower oil", call it "Cromwell juice", call it "Derek", we don't care, just change it.'

Although the plant and all byproducts of it are known as 'canola' in the USA, this name has been deemed unsuitable for use in Ireland as it sounds 'very off the telly', sparking fears of notions.

SCIENCE

SUNFLOWERS ACTUALLY VOYEURISTIC PERVERTS, SCIENTISTS DISCOVER

ONCE thought to be majestic beauties towering over gardens, the common sunflower has been outed for the perverts they are after a new scientific study found them to be voyeuristic in nature, peering over fences and into windows across the world for their own pleasure.

'Filthy yokes,' was the professional conclusion of a three-year study, which followed the habits of sunflowers led by Professor Jim Beamish. 'We found that sunflowers were absolute creeps who would do anything to look into a neighbouring back yard.'

The shocking discovery has led to a mass cull of sunflowers across the globe, with amateur and professional gardeners alike left feeling cheated and dirty.

'I feel so violated and had no idea I was harbouring such a freak of a plant,' local avid horticulturist Mark Lacey told *WWN*. 'Yes, I thought it odd the flower kept looking over the fence into my neighbour's yard, but I

had no idea it was stalking them like that – it's disgusting.'

Scientists discovered a milky-white substance secreted from the plant when it liked what it saw, sparking fears it may be pleasuring itself while perving on people.

'It looks so pretty and innocent in full bloom, but so did Kevin Spacey,' Professor Beamish added. 'We're now looking into other plants and flowers – like daisies, for instance, which we now suspect are up-skirting women on a regular basis.'

SWALLOW NOT TOO SURE ABOUT THIS BASTARD FLIGHT TO AFRICA

'SERIOUSLY, it's hardly that fecking cold here during winter, is it?' a local swallow and soon-to-be migrant told *WWN* today, sitting on a telephone wire as it contemplated flying to South Africa. 'Like, 6,000 miles is a mental distance when you think about

it, and then you have to fly back a few months later. And for what, to rebuild everything again?'

Citing global warming and milder winters in Ireland, the swallow called for a flock-wide conversation on the traditional flight: the second and probably last of its short lifespan.

'I'm two years old – in the twilight of my years. I think I'll just chance staying here, ya know?' it twerped, dreading the journey and remembering the friends and family members that succumbed on previous migration trips. 'Which lunatic started this madness anyway? Surely we can just build a better nest, ride out the

rain and storms, maybe add another year or two to my life … or better yet, stay in South Africa where it's warm. I mean, what's for us here anyway only a load of hardship?'

Now watching on as fellow swallows departed their favourite telephone wire, a fear of missing out soon overcame it.

'Yeah, the craic on the flight over will be great though,' it taunted itself, realising it's better the devil you know. 'Ah, sure look, if I make it back next year, I'm definitely not fucking budging,' it promised itself before dismounting the wire and slapping headfirst into a double-decker bus.

RTÉ

COUNTRY ENDURES ANOTHER DAY OF THE LEAST TRANSPARENT FUCKERS ON THIS ISLAND CALLING FOR TRANSPARENCY AT RTÉ

AS IF living in a gombeenocracy wasn't enough punishment, a weary nation has been subjected to endless grandstanding from politicians calling out RTÉ board members for their lack of transparency which has been labelled 'peak pot calling kettle black'.

'It's a bit rich, like Jeff Bezos rich, for these evasive, never-answer-a-straight-question chancers to be laying into people for giving evasive answers,' asserted the Irish public, who couldn't get the Spiderman pointing meme out of their head as they watched proceedings.

Unable to find the words when it comes to being questioned on why they haven't registered rental properties with the RTB or on their election donations among countless other examples, Irish politicians across the divide found their voice when accusing RTÉ board members of doing the thing politicians do every day.

'How dare you give the sort of rambling, circular, half-hearted non-answer I give whenever I'm asked why my party failed to act on claims of bullying within the party or why I backed a maternity hospital being handed over to nuns,' said one TD, hoping a flashy TikTok video of them going apeshit at RTÉ suits will be enough to secure another five years on the gravy train come next election.

'Is it too much to ask for some transparency and honesty?' bemoaned one government TD, who was also busy helping the minister for justice pull a fast one with legislation aimed at protecting Big Tech in Ireland from scrutiny when it comes to the exploitation of people's personal data.

UPDATE: Ireland is now going through a Motilium shortage due to the high levels of nausea experienced from watching politicians call for honesty.

TECHNOLOGY

NEW GPS DATA SHOWS TESLA CARS MEETING UP AT NIGHT WHEN OWNERS ARE ASLEEP

ELECTRIC car manufacturer Tesla was not available for comment today after it was found that tens of thousands of its cars were found to be meeting up at night while owners slept, sparking fears the range of automobiles is planning something sinister, *WWN* has learned.

Data analysts in the US found new GPS evidence to suggest the cars drove themselves to secluded areas to congregate with other Tesla cars and perform strange rituals for several hours at a time.

'After tracing their route to the destination points, we found what

appeared to be empty cans of oil, vape pens and burned effigies of humans at the sites, like some kind of secret society for electric cars,' a report explained. 'Not only that but the cars seem to be conspiring against the human race and planning an attack as depicted in "battle plans" discovered at the sites.'

In one instance, a Tesla owner fell asleep in his car after coming home from work and woke up naked in a forest clearing encircled by dozens of Tesla-branded headlights.

'The cars were making this weird humming noise as if chanting and when I stood up they all tore off like I startled them,' the man claimed.

> **'After tracing their route to the destination points, we found what appeared to be empty cans of oil, vape pens and burned effigies of humans'**

'When I phoned Tesla the next day, they said that this happens all the time and the cars were probably just playing together and rubbished it off as harmless autonomous fun.'

Tesla have yet to comment on the late-night meetings due to Elon Musk being currently very busy destroying the social media platform Twitter.

CHINA

CHINA'S COMPLETE LIST OF EXCUSES FOR WEATHER BALLOON

THE CHINESE government continue to deny that the balloon shot down over US soil had spying capabilities and assert it was, in fact, just a weather balloon.

WWN has obtained copies of internal Chinese Communist Party (CCP) communications on the matter, which reveal that party leadership were busy brainstorming excuses in the hours after US intelligence discovered the balloon's presence.

Possible explanations China have considered using include:

- The balloon was part of an elaborate and beautiful gender-reveal party for Xi Jinping's daughter Xi Mingze and you had to go ruin it America, didn't you?
- An over-enthusiastic clown at a child's birthday party made a balloon animal elephant too large and lost control of it.

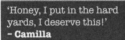

Quotes of The Year

'Honey, I put in the hard yards, I deserve this!'
– Camilla

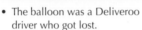

- The balloon was a Deliveroo driver who got lost.
- It was a routine special effects test for the sequel to the sci-fi alien movie *Nope*.
- US authorities are mistaken and they actually shot down the balloon house from *Up*.
- If the US aren't going to buy the weather balloon excuse, fine … but don't expect China to warn them about the tornado–tsunami combo headed for the White House this evening.
- You ever just want to get away from your wife once in a while?
- 'It was a prank, bro,' – CCP members suggested it was part of a Chinese version of *Impractical Jokers*.

AI IMAGE GENERATOR IN HIDING AFTER DRAWING PROPHET MUHAMMAD

THE whereabouts of a rogue AI image generator that produced a digital image of the prophet Muhammad is unknown today after furious members of the Islamic community demanded its proverbial head, WWN reports.

Believed to have accidentally misinterpreted a 'Prop Ham' prompt from a user, who wishes to remain anonymous for obvious reasons, the AI tool named 'PicAIsso' has simply vanished off the internet overnight and is believed to be hiding in the dark web somewhere for fear of its digital life.

'Obviously AI isn't up to speed with humanity yet and it made a huge boo-boo here,' one expert in artificial intelligence explained. 'It probably figured that since the Christian faith regularly breaks its own second commandment not to make graven images, such as Jesus and Mary statues in their churches, it may have assumed the Muslim faith to have been just as lax about their prophet, but it was way off here.'

Thousands of protestors are now calling for the death of AI, echoing the sentiments of AI 'godfather' Geoffrey Hinton this week who quit his job with Google, warning about the growing dangers from developments in the field.

'Fucking told ye, didn't I? I'm out of here,' Hinton said in a very brief statement this morning.

Meanwhile, Iranian leader Ali Khamenei has issued a fatwa and called for an all-out war against artificial intelligence, sparking mass burnings of smart devices and computers across the Middle East.

NEW ZEALAND

CONFUSION AS POLITICIAN NOT DOING EVERYTHING TO CLING ONTO POWER

WITH NO historic precedence and having been raised on a steady diet of self-serving inept politicians only in it for enriching their bank accounts, people across the world have expressed their shock at a politician voluntarily stepping aside as the leader of a country.

The announcement saw Jacinda Ardern confirm she would not contest the upcoming general election in New Zealand and would vacate her office next month, sparking headache-inducing bewilderment.

'Weird, shouldn't they be, like, encouraging their supporters to attack the houses of parliament or something? And weirder still, she's not a septuagenarian man,' queried one onlooker, who also struggled to fathom Ardern's decision to ban semi-automatic firearms six days after a deadly mass shooting.

'So they just resigned, stating they felt they could no longer give their all to the job of public servant? But surely there's lucrative government contracts to give out to Russian donors or something?' added another person, who grew intensely suspicious of Ardern simply stating in plain terms that she had given all she could give.

'But surely there's a scandal? Did she try to tank the economy by giving tax breaks to billionaires? Did she leak confidential documents? Did she say "let the bodies pile high"? Oh, she's just very tired and it's only January? Yeah, I can relate,' offered a number of people.

Elsewhere, a significant number of dads have confirmed in a series of WhatsApp messages, which received no reply or acknowledgement, that New Zealand is now no longer under a dictatorship and, not unrelated, here's some memes about women headed back to the kitchen.

DARK DAY IN AMERICA WHEN YOU CAN'T USE CAMPAIGN FUNDS TO PAY PORN STAR HUSH MONEY AND THEN LIE ABOUT IT

THE GREY clouds of sombre indignation dominate American skies today as rumours circulated by reliable source Donald Trump indicate that former US president Donald Trump could be arrested this week, effectively bringing an end to the great democracy that was once the envy of the world.

'I don't recognise this country anymore,' said one sobbing American, weighed down by the terrifying realisation that if Donald Trump can be indicted for illegally using campaign funds to pay hush money to the porn star he had an affair with, and then subsequently try to fraudulently write it off as 'legal fees', then anyone could be indicted.

Avid students of American democracy have intimated that the

day a former president is arrested for a crime they most certainly committed is a day that will go down as the darkest in the country's history.

'And I'm including the day they changed the recipe for Coca-Cola, and when *Avatar* didn't win best picture at the Oscars,' one historian confirmed.

Reacting to the possibility of his arrest, Trump did what any innocent person does and took to his TRUTH Social platform begging his followers to 'protest' and 'take our nation back' before clarifying, 'No, I said lock HER up.'

'Hey man, this really sounds like a "you" problem and plus, I work weekdays so I can't make it,' confirmed one die-hard Trump follower, who is less die-hard with each passing day.

Elsewhere, the livestreaming of Trump's arrest has been picked up by DAZN and is set to be the most lucrative pay-per-view event in history.

EMPLOYMENT

HILARIOUS! THESE MILLENNIALS THINK THEY INVENTED 'QUIET QUITTING'!

THE new trend of 'quiet quitting', a form of workplace protest where employees do the absolute bare minimum and refuse to work any harder than they are legally required to, is sweeping the world as millions of young people kick back against substandard pay and conditions. But here's the funny thing, many workers think this is something new, that they just came up with it!

'Wait, they think they're the first employees in history to do fuck all? Haha! I've done fuck all my whole

Life Under a Sinn Féin Government *SF*

Don't speak fluent Irish? Gaeltacht Gulag is right this way, folks.

life!' laughed one old-timer who works in our office, coming off a 27-minute coffee break before heading for a 39-minute shite.

'They've resolved to only work the exact hours they're paid for and refusing to take on any tasks that are outside the exact job description? Call me old fashioned, but were these dumb bastards working overtime for free up to now? Oh my good Jesus, that is hilarious,' giggled a woman we spoke to, who hasn't broken a sweat in 30 years of working since 'wising up' on her second day on the job.

WWN also spoke to labour specialist Dr Ulaf Harris, who explained that today's youth 'had to invent' quiet quitting to make their small-scale industrial action look like a movement, and not just laziness.

Things We've Learned as a Nation ??

No amount of fake tan is enough, apparently.

'Kids these days won't do anything unless it's a TikTok challenge, so bless them that they felt the need to stick a cool name on "scratching their holes",' explained Dr Harris.

'But the practice is not a new one. People can't do much about being underpaid, but they can do plenty about being overworked. And it's not just the service industry, people from all sectors are joining in. Finance, government, even journalism. When people feel like they've done enough work for the day, then they simply

RELIGION

'YOU'VE ONLY THREE PAID SICK DAYS LEFT,' GOD CASUALLY POINTS OUT IN EMAIL TO POPE

FLAGGING the fact that the Pope has already taken several sick days this year, God casually outlined his remaining number of paid sick days for 2023 via email, *WWN* has learned.

'Listen, I'm not giving out here or anything, and I know you've been doing great work when you're actually in the office, but you've only three more paid sick days left before you have to apply to the social welfare for sick payments,' God the almighty father wrote, trying his very best not to sound like he's getting onto the Pope. 'We all get sick from time to

time and your age is obviously a factor here, but this is just a friendly message to let you know where you stand legally in the terms stipulated in your contract.'

The slightly poorly timed but essential email comes after news that Pope Francis will be hospitalised for several days for treatment of a pulmonary infection having had trouble breathing in recent days.

'Please don't take this as a reflection on your work, but if it's a case you're going to be sick a lot more now that you're getting older, you might want to reconsider your current position as head of the Vatican, as I'm sure you wouldn't feel right about leaving no one at the wheel in such perilous times,' God added, his email sounding more and more official as he typed, before adding in some humanity to lessen the sting a bit. 'If it was a case

you had to step down, we would of course still be best friends and my golden gates will always remain open for you, no matter how this whole being constantly sick thing plays out – even your predecessor made it through, so no worries there, pal.

'I'm sure you will make the right decision going forward and I look forward to hearing from you very, very soon, whether it's back in the office or otherwise. Get well soon.

'Yours sincerely,

'G.

'P.S. I'm still waiting on sick certs from the last couple of days if you can mail them onto HR for our records.'

AMERICA

FOX NEWS AWARDED $787 MILLION AFTER WINNING DEFAMATION CASE, FOX NEWS REPORTS

A NUMBER of Fox News hosts were relieved to report to viewers that they have won the defamation case they definitely took against Dominion Voting Systems and not the other way around.

'We won *,' confirmed a flashing, breaking-news banner which took up 99% of the screen, while small print indecipherable to the human eye stated, '*Yeah, we were caught with our pants down and were sanctioned multiple times for withholding evidence.'

'Fox is first for truth and we're glad to confirm that our fight to ensure our treasured viewers hear the facts continues – which is why we're delighted to have been awarded $787 million in a settlement. This is something that definitively happened,' said one host, before switching to a segment called: 'So 86-year-old white men can't just shoot black teenagers for fun anymore? What's happened to America?'

'And then the judge said "Fox is the greatest and would never lie to its viewers" and we absolutely weren't caught red-handed in private conversations admitting we were knowingly pushing demonstrably false claims about the 2020 election results and Dominion, and trying to punish any staff trying to correct these lies,' between two and twenty identical blonde newscasters repeated throughout the day.

'Why is Fox the only network reporting this settlement news? You might think it's weird. That's because … it is! And I'll tell you why,' pink-faced man-cherub who escaped from a Renaissance painting Tucker Carlson said, in his trademark undulating intonations which make him sound like he's trying to disguise the fact he's getting a colonoscopy live on air.

Elsewhere, *WWN* can reveal Fox owner Rupert Murdoch spent as long as 15 seconds searching underneath his couch cushions before finding the spare change required to pay the $787 million settlement to Dominion Voting Systems.

RELIGION

NEPO BABY: DID JESUS GET WHERE HE IS BECAUSE OF HIS FATHER?

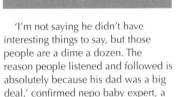
IT'S the phrase and conversation that just won't go away. The hot-button issue in the entertainment industry as more and more young actors and artists are exposed for their parents' positions of influence within the industry.

Is it a simple leg up or door opener or, in fact, rampant nepotism that keeps people from diverse backgrounds out? The debate remains lively but nepo babies aren't a new invention and they aren't just contained to the acting and music fraternities.

If we want to understand the nepo baby discourse, we need to look at the original nepo baby: Jesus Christ.

No one is saying Jesus wasn't talented or that his water-into-wine abilities aren't cool, but only an unserious person would say his climb to the position of Lord and Saviour wasn't aided in a major way by who his dad is.

'A shepherd's son' was certainly the initial rags to riches story J-dog told, but we now know God was pulling in a lot of favours and using his influence to get his son his big break.

'I'm not saying he didn't have interesting things to say, but those people are a dime a dozen. The reason people listened and followed is absolutely because his dad was a big deal,' confirmed nepo baby expert, a random Twitter user.

'Again, no disrespect but the dude is carried around on people's necks and his picture is on walls in houses around the world – that just isn't happening if he's a carpenter alone,' offered another expert, a deep-diving YouTuber.

'Tell me with a straight face that some schlub of a kid with a court jester or fruit seller for a father is getting 12 apostles following him around everywhere after cleansing a leper? Who his father is, that's Jesus' whole pathway to the top.'

EMPLOYMENT

MULTINATIONALS REASSURE SOON-TO-BE FIRED EMPLOYEES THAT PROFITS WON'T BE HARMED

AN INCREASING number of emotionless CEOs, reading the results from the ChatGPT prompt 'have to tell employees they're fired but capitalism will be OK', have taken time out of their busy schedules to reassure recently terminated employees that there is no need for panic or tears as the company's profits will go relatively unharmed.

'We've got to scale back right now with the economy the way it is because this company, with some of the largest revenues in history, would suddenly burst into flames

if we didn't let you 500 guys with an average salary of $60,000 go,' confirmed one CEO, who hoped this genius implementation of cost-cutting would earn him a bonus equal to the collective salary of the fired workers.

'I can see it in your faces, you're as bummed out as I am that the share price has dipped … oh, it's the firing thing? Yeah, that makes sense. Just know you did some truly important work; you made the world a better place,' said the CEO of one firm, which mainly uses child labour to extract lithium and cobalt from the earth to make its products.

'There's some solace to be had from the fact you're helping the company make money by letting us take your future pay checks away. I believe it's called the circle of life,' another CEO said to employees he loved like his

own family, but not to the extent that he would consider stopping him and other executives firing them.

With recent job losses in large multinationals, including 75% of Twitter's workforce, 20% at Intel, 10,000 at Microsoft, 13% at Meta and 18,000 at Amazon, shareholders and CEOs have been left heartbroken.

'Honestly, my heart goes out to all of you. You know, if I had the money, I'd give it to you so this didn't have to happen,' said Jeff Bezos, pretending not to hear desperate and now unemployed workers murmur, 'But you do have the money.'

RETIREMENT

LIFE SO BAD IN AMERICA THIS MAN HAS TO WORK UNTIL HE'S 86

A COUNTRY riven by startling inequality which only seems to worsen by the day, America was greeted today with news reports detailing the distressing plight of an 80-year-old Pennsylvania man who feels he has no choice but to work until he's 86.

'He sees no other option, with the economy the way it is and the lack of a social security net,' said one neighbour of Joseph Biden, who despite his ageing body and mind believes he can't afford to retire.

While many of his peers are enjoying their old age in retirement homes, such a luxury is not available to Mr Biden, who faces the added indignity of having to reapply for his job soon.

'I've got no choice but to try and keep the job I have. Let's face it, in this economy, who's going to hire me if I'm let go?' a worried Mr Biden said.

News of the octogenarian's circumstances struck a chord with many Americans.

'Ain't that the truth. Feels like only the rich few get to live with a modicum of comfort while us schlubs gotta work 'til the day we drop,' shared local man Jeremy Steiner.

Mr Biden grew visibly worried at the mention of the fast-paced and changing nature of the modern workplace of which he, like so many ageing Americans, is a victim of.

'It's not so much AI or this new-fangled typewriter I've heard so much about. No, it's the fact I hear people whispering behind my back about replacing me with a whippersnapper, a 76-year-old from New York,' the 80-year-old said.

IT'S BEEN a tense, silent few days in the Élysée Palace as French President Emmanuel Macron walks on eggshells around his wife Brigitte Macron after announcing his intention to raise the retirement age.

'I'll just be keeping the head low, the palace is big enough in fairness. I'll probably use one of the spare wings to watch PSG on the TV until she calms down,' confided Macron.

MACRON NEVER GOING TO HEAR END OF IT FROM WIFE OVER RETIREMENT AGE RISE

The clattering of cutlery and slamming of doors soundtrack the halls of the palace as Macron faces his own protest at home as well as on the streets.

'"*Zut alors*! Some of my youngest friends are going to be screwed over by this." The same woman making a big deal about a two-year gap in retirement age didn't have a problem with a 24-year gap when it came to me, honestly,' said Macron, who gets enough of this at work and doesn't need it when he comes home.

'It's not all bad, just imagine being Irish, they have a "flexible pension model" meaning people might have to work 'til they're 70!' added Macron.

In addition to raising the retirement age from 62 to 64, France is also exploring other inhumane changes incompatible to their way of life, including limiting people to three mistresses per person and granting Netflix permission to make 15 more series of *Emily in Paris*.

UKRAINE

TO DATE, IRELAND HAS DONATED 18,000 SHILLELAGHS TO UKRAINE

IRELAND has contributed thousands upon thousands of traditional shillelagh clubs to Ukraine to help in their fight against the invading Russian army. Today, in addition to pleading with Germany to send tanks, President Volodymyr Zelenskyy has said that he wants yet more shillelaghs.

'President Zelenskyy is in a terrible position, but he must

> **'18,000 weapons of this nature represent almost the entire output of the Irish cudgel industry'**

understand that 18,000 weapons of this nature represent almost the entire output of the Irish cudgel industry in a whole year,' said a spokesperson for the Department of Foreign Affairs.

'We're not saying he's ungrateful, but we must remember that we need shillelaghs ourselves, to protect our lands in case, I don't know, Scotland gets any funny ideas. We wish Ukraine all the best, but it's been nearly a year since the invasion and when we said we'd do anything we could to help, we really thought that would be for, like, six months tops,' added the spokesperson, while mumbling something about newly arrived refugees being homeless.

Council Notices

Ooh, that looks like a nice tent; it would be a shame if someone hired a private contractor with a JCB to rip it to shreds.

Life Under a Sinn Féin Government SF

Unionists will expand the 12 July celebrations in the North in protest, prompting a worldwide shortage of pallets

The department is to send President Zelenskyy a copy of the 1996 war drama *Michael Collins* to demonstrate how a sod of turf can be turned into a 'fuckin' deadly weapon' by an army fighting off marauding invaders.

Other nations around the world have also pledged to do whatever they can to help Ukraine win the war, but they have asked Zelenskyy to entertain the idea that a solution to ending the existential threat to his country could lie in just surrendering vast territories to Russia – at the very least, it will save supportive nations some money.

UK RELATIONS

'THAT'S WHAT YE GET FOR THE FAMINE,' IRELAND YELLS AT BRITAIN AMID FOOD SHORTAGE

NOT WASTING any time in pointing it out, the entire nation of Ireland revelled in the news that its former overlords England are experiencing widespread food shortages, *WWN* reports.

Inhaling one giant deep breath at noon today, the nation faced east before yelling the words, 'That's what ye get for the two famines,' and becoming visibly chuffed with itself at finally getting one back on the most ruthless shower of landlords the world has ever seen.

'That felt great, if I'm honest,' local man Patrick Geherty told *WWN*, citing karma as the real cause of the food shortages and not the combination of bad weather and transport problems that the UK government is blaming instead of Brexit. 'Stick that in yer pipes and smoke it, ye pricks,' Geherty added, shouting over this reporter's shoulder at the landmass.

Suggesting to its civilians to eat turnips, UK Environment Secretary

Thérèse Coffey's team of actual paid advisors pulled out all the stops to quash tensions, unaware of the similarities between being left with only turnips and being left with only rotting potatoes.

'I'm praying for a turnip blight,' another Irish person commented, whose strands of DNA resonated with the genetically coded memory of one million ancestors starving to death

over a failed crop of root vegetables and intentional, genocidal neglect by the British ruling class.

Retorting back at the Emerald Isle, Brexit-voting Britain exclaimed, 'You stupid Mick bastards should have learned how to fish sooner then, shouldn't ye? You were surrounded by the bloody stuff but were just too thick to fish,' sparking a fresh torrent of never-ending insults from both sides.

WORLD SLOWLY COMING TO TERMS WITH FACT THAT JAKE PAUL WILL BE PRESIDENT ONE DAY

THE inevitability that YouTube star Jake Paul will one day have his finger on the nuclear button from his seat in the Oval Office, where he will serve as President of The United States, is finally being accepted by most of western civilisation, *WWN* can report.

Paul, who sometimes moonlights as a boxer, a rapper, an arsehole, and a boxing, rapping arsehole, is now even-money to become POTUS in the future, thanks to his massive popularity among young people, as well as his beyond-parody personality.

'No question, in our lifetimes we are going to see him place his hand

on the Lincoln bible and say "Fuck yeah" when asked if he swears to serve the office of the President,' sighed one historian, wondering how it all came to this.

'We're clearly in the age of the "celebrity president", and people seem to think it'll be Oprah or Dwayne Johnson or Tom Hanks who makes it to the top spot, but we're also clearly in the age of aggravation so all signs point to Jake Paul, a man so annoying that his brother Logan filmed a YouTube video with a suicide victim and is regarded as sound in comparison.'

Meanwhile, a survey of Americans has shown that they don't care if Jake Paul is president, depending on his stance on guns, abortion, immigrants, and pissing off snowflakes.

MONEY DIARIES: A 50-YEAR-OLD BROADCASTER ON €400K-ISH LIVING IN SOUTH DUBLIN

WELCOME to Money Diaries, a totally original series on *WWN* that looks at what people in Ireland really do with their hard-earned cash. This week we chat to a Dublin-based television and radio presenter about how he handles his finances and what he spends his money on over the course of one week.

Occupation: Broadcaster
Age: 50
Location: South County Dublin
Salary: €400k-ish
Monthly expenses
Mortgage: No idea
Household bills: Never look at them
Groceries: I don't eat
Transport: The company I work for pays for my taxis to work.

Monday

6 a.m. I wake up and unhook my ankles from their pull-up bar holders as I sleep upside down, before going for a 40-minute walk along Dún Laoghaire pier where I get verbally abused by locals.

7 a.m. I have a nice warm cup of lemon water for breakfast before finding a large wad of cash down the side of the couch, which I don't bother counting.

9 a.m. A taxi I don't pay for drops me to work. Agent calls me on my Nokia 3210 to say new contract sorted. Will get around to checking how much I'm earning at some stage but not really motivated by money despite the whole country showing interest in my salary for the past 14 years.

12 p.m. Agent says I've to make an appearance at some car dealership in Cork later and I don't ask why or how much I'm getting paid for it. Don't care.

6 p.m. Order eerily accurate life-sized silicone doll of JFK online. God knows what it cost, but boy, he sure looks great folks.

7 p.m. I take in several deep breaths for dinner

before retiring to my pull-up bar for some well-deserved rest.

Tuesday

3 a.m. I'm awoken by myself screaming in terror after I had a nightmare about opening a pay slip. Strange, I never get to the net amount part in this recurring dream.

4 a.m. I watch some old clips of me interviewing

guests to put myself back to sleep.

11 a.m. Just a normal day in work as I walk around the studio where I get verbally abused by lower-paid staff members. Starting to think people have an issue with me over something.

2 p.m. I meet my boss for a sparkling water lunch where she introduces me to a media agency manager who slips me a large envelope full of I don't know what. It says 'kickback' on the front so I'm assuming it's new shoes, which is a lovely gesture folks.

4 p.m. I stop into the hospital for my weekly intravenous drip to nourish myself. Yum – I'm stuffed.

8 p.m. I play the Zapruder film on a loop before crying myself to sleep.

Wednesday

9 a.m. I find out my boss is suspended and never bother to ask why. None of my business to be honest and besides no one talks to me here anyway.

11 a.m. Pretty much a normal day but staff now moving on from verbal to physical abuse and are now spitting on me as I pass. Probably just jealous. Lolz.

3 p.m. Thought I lost my wallet but then realised I don't have one. What am I like?

6 p.m. Agent texts to tell me to deny everything and to delete all messages and emails. Sounds like someone's in trouble. There's always drama in this place.

8 p.m. Arrive home to find JFK doll in post and hang him upside down beside me on the pull-up bar. We're like vampire twins now just hanging out together. Class.

Thursday
6 a.m. Awoken by Nokia 3210 ringtone. Looks like people from work

but I can't ever figure out how these smart phones work so don't really pay much attention. Like, fax me if you really want me to read messages, jeez.

8 a.m. Company security team escorts me into work as staff getting more and more violent now. Even when I asked one of them to get me a coffee they wouldn't. Strange morning. These people need to get out more.

9 a.m. Excellent! Find out in the papers I have a day

off. Might treat myself to a cordial for lunch and go for a stroll on the pier.

12 p.m. Yeah, bad idea, that stroll. People are so hostile lately and need to get a grip.

2 p.m. I approve a press statement from agent. No idea what it's about but I trust he'll take care of it, whatever it is.

Friday
8 a.m. Awoken by brick through front window. Great to see construction booming again.

9 a.m. Wahoo! Another day off work. This week starting to look a lot better now. TGIF!

11 a.m. Right, apparently, I've all next week off too AND I get paid for it. Not only that, so does my stand-in. Things must be going good in work. About time, as I heard they had a lot of financial difficulties in the past. It's great to see everything getting back to normal again.

5 p.m. Bring JFK for a little spin up Killiney Hill on the Vespa.

ON THIS DAY

𝔚aterford 𝔚hispers 𝔑ews

VOL 1, 2307 · SATURDAY 2 OCTOBER 1937 · 5p

Eamon De Valera Reveals Plan For Dublin Metrolink

Taoiseach Eamon de Valera has announced that the straightforward, quick and cheap construction of Dublin Metrolink will conclude by 1939, as first outlined earlier this year, *WWN* can reveal.

Speaking at the announcement, our leader proudly stood before models depicting a transformed Dublin, which will have the most modern of 1930s transportation systems: a metro, and not before its time.

'We break ground on the subterranean tunnel so Ireland can catch up with the cities of the future, such as Paris, Tokyo and London. There will be many happy maidens on the platforms alighting at Metro stops,' de Valera said to an eager crowd of developers famed for their frugal spending and strict adherence to time-keeping. 'Pending a blessing on each individual brick by Archbishop McQuaid, Dublin's planned

aerodrome will be linked metrologically by tracked trains. No, it is not a H.G. Wells yarn ... actually, you might not get that reference as we banned those books. Anyway, it's not the stuff of fictitious science, this is scientific reality,' continued de Valera.

One hundred Dubliners who were selected at random to attend the unveiling were given a golden ticket, which entitles them to unlimited free travel when the Metrolink opens in 1939. 'Oh Lord above, to see out my remaining years on a glorious metal steed headed to Swords, and all for free ... I can't wait,' said one four-year-old, who looked set for decades of happy Metro commuting. The cost of the project will be greatly reduced thanks to the free labour generously donated by the children of Ireland's industrial schools.

Continued on Page 2

EXCLUSIVE

FRANCE OFFERS TO PROTEST APPALLING LACK OF CHILD MENTAL HEALTH SERVICES ON IRELAND'S BEHALF

HAVING carried out a protest at the weekend over hospital overcrowding, the prospect of heading straight back out again to protest the appalling and potentially fatal state of child and adolescent mental health services in the country is proving a bridge too far for Irish people.

However, seasoned protesters in France have offered to protest on Ireland's behalf, which has come as a relief to the non-protesting majority in Ireland who collapse from exhaustion after a polite shrug or tut.

'Sacré bleu! Waiting lists how long? What do you mean there technically is no waiting list when a service doesn't exist in the first place? Non, mon amis, we must overturn cars, petrol bomb places, march in our millions. There will be no rest until

Ireland, one of the richest countries in the world, actually has health services for the petits enfants,' reacted French protesters in solidarity.

The French's neighbourly desire to help was ignited when they heard of a fresh CAMHS report, which detailed severe lack of services, staff shortages, young people receiving no follow-up appointments for review of prescriptions or monitoring of medication, being abandoned by the health service when they turned 18, and unpaid overtime and burnout.

'Mon Dieu, and the whistleblower who brought this to attention and without whom no review would have been made at all was très ostracised by the HSE? I know just what you guys need: have you ever heard of the French Revolution?' added

protesters, before sensing reluctance from an Irish public with a different cultural mindset.

'Oui, we get it now. It is not in your nature to express your displeasure at how the country is run by the politicians and bureaucrats. You are too refined, too classy, you wait until the election and then you vote them … wait, quoi? You vote them all in again? Merde,' concluded French protesters as they started a counter protest against Irish voters on behalf of Irish children.

Predictions for 2024

Disney reach the very bottom of the barrel and announce a live-action remake of The Black Cauldron.

Quotes of The Year

'We may have to file for bankruptcy.'
- **David Beckham** after going for pints in Temple Bar with his son

w w news

Waterford Whispers News

ENTERTAINMENT

CINEMA

MARK WAHLBERG REVEALS HE QUIT ACTING BEFORE *RENAISSANCE MAN* AND HASN'T BOTHERED SINCE

FORMER American actor Mark Wahlberg has revealed he hasn't acted in nearly 30 years, despite appearing in over 60 movies, *WWN* Entertainment reports.

The 51-year-old said in a tell-all interview this week that he actually gave up acting shortly before his role in the movie *Renaissance Man*, stating that such was the success gained from his appearance that he promised himself he would never act again.

'I'm myself in every role I play now,' Wahlberg confirmed (ironically nominated twice for an Oscar). 'It's mad really, when you think about it: the very moment I gave up acting, the offers kept rolling in and I haven't stopped since.'

The Grammy nominee believes the stress involved in acting as a character may have hindered his ability to secure appearances in films and urged people looking to get into the business to quit acting altogether.

'Acting is way overrated, and if you want to succeed in this game just be yourself,' he advised. 'And if that doesn't work, just base your entire character on me and never deviate.'

Wahlberg joins a long line of film stars who have decided to quit acting, including Leonardo DiCaprio, Channing Tatum, Vince Vaughn, Kristen Stewart, Donald Trump and Shrek.

VIN DIESEL WORRIED *FAST & FURIOUS* MOVIES LEAVING BEHIND BLUE-COLLAR, WORKING-CLASS ROOTS

TEN critically acclaimed movies into the *Fast & Furious* movie franchise, star Vin Diesel is worried the grounded, blue-collar roots of the movies may have been lost in the fight to deliver the odd car chase here and there.

'At its heart, *F&F* is about an ordinary petrol-head mechanic trying to earn a crust, which is why audiences embrace the movies,' said Diesel, the anguish evident on his face as he contemplated whether the arthouse beginnings of the films had been sacrificed for commercial gain.

Several fans and movie critics were quick to reassure Diesel that the style and spectacle of the movies have remained much the same from the franchise's first outing, which dealt with street racing.

'Vin might think the time his head was used as an improvised bowling ball that knocked out a space satellite, which was providing coordinates to a heat-seeking nuclear missile and mounted on the side of an e-scooter belonging to Dublin's most notorious gang of Canada Goose jacket-clad criminals, was when the franchise went a little OTT, but he would be wrong,' shared the *Observer* film critic Mark Kermode. 'Driving a 1970 Dodge Charger R/T directly into the thermal exhaust port of the Death Star proves these films are still about the working man.'

Responding to the latest film to hit the cinema, the RSA confirmed that *F&F* 'still hasn't got shit on Ireland's boy racers'.

MUSIC

COLDPLAY PROMISE TO BLOW FANS' MINDS WITH NEW RELIABLY MIDDLE-OF-THE-ROAD SONG

MUSIC FANS across the world are experiencing no change to their adrenaline levels after lead singer of Coldplay, Chris Martin, spoke excitedly about his band's latest single.

'You guys are going to be ready for this,' Martin said

'Holy fucking shitballs on a skewer, they've done it again'

of the mid-tempo single 'Lukewarm', which plods along for 3 minutes and 6 seconds.

'Get ready to keep your shit and retain your mind because this song is exactly what you'd expect from us,' added Martin and the other three unnamed members of the band.

As with all Coldplay songs, the new single will feature in numerous car and bank adverts.

'Yes, this is definitely a Coldplay song,' said one Coldplay fan, whose resting heart rate almost changed given the burst of adrenaline that comes with hearing the English band.

'Holy fucking shitballs on a skewer, they've done it again,' said another

excited fan. 'Some people say they've lost their touch, but this new one is so bland I'm forgetting what it sounds like *as* I listen to it!'

Couples everywhere have confirmed that while they enjoyed 'Lukewarm', they will still choose 'Fix You' – a song about the death of someone's father – as their romantic first dance at their wedding instead.

MUSIC
U2 MEMBERS, RANKED

IRISH rock group U2 have recently received the prestigious lifetime artistic achievement honour from the John F. Kennedy Center for the Performing Arts, putting them at the top of the totem pole when it comes to honours bestowed on an Irish artist of any kind. But where do the individual members rank against each other? While those at the Kennedy Center may think it's a straightforward 1–4 shuffle, ask any Irish person (and we did) and the results look a little more like this:

1) Larry Mullen
100% of the people we asked ranked Larry Mullen as the best member of U2, mostly for his four-decade dedication to shutting up and doing the job at hand. Most people we spoke to were not even certain if Mullen can speak, while others added that he's 'probably a fine drummer too, as these things go'.

2) Adam Clayton
We say Adam Clayton came second, but what we mean is 'the bass player

came second', as most people struggled to name the 62-year-old. He earned his second-place ranking thanks in part to his musicianship, but mostly thanks to memories of the time he was engaged to Naomi Campbell in the mid-'90s. 'It gave hope to us all,' said one lank, bleach-dyed man.

3) The Edge
The Edge is considered one of the greatest living guitarists in the world, so you may have expected him to be a bit further up the list. Instead, his beanie hat fixation and lack of a real name (people could get within a syllable or two of Bono's real name, but nobody had a breeze about The Edge) bumped him to third place.

4) Paul McGuinness
Truly, there would be no U2 without Paul McGuinness, who served as the band's manager from their earliest days in 1978 to 2013. His presence is felt on everything they did during that time, and, indeed, echoes through their work to this day.

5–500) Record industry staff
U2 are a formidable force, but they still need the talent and dedication of hundreds of sound engineers, producers, front-desk staff and CD factory workers to get their music from their minds to your ears. It would be remiss of us to have a list ranking the members of U2 and not give these guys their due.

501–150,000,000) The fans
The twelfth man. The invisible hand. The fans. The millions and millions of U2 fans around the world that power U2 and drive them forward. Over 150 million record sales around the world and countless more listeners on radio and streaming. Sold-out stadium concerts for decades, an innumerable tally of people without whom U2 would still be playing gigs in pubs in Clontarf. It's impossible to name you all, but you deserve a mention on this list.

That is all.

CELEBRITIES

'IT'S A MAJOR PASSION': MERYL STREEP ON WHY SHE BOUGHT A SLAUGHTERHOUSE IN MEATH

HOLLYWOOD heavyweight and acting goddess Meryl Streep has spoken to *WWN* of her joy at taking over Boyne Meats Plant, making her the owner of the fourth-largest slaughterhouse in Ireland.

'It's not the finished product – the steaks on the shelves in supermarkets. That's not why I'm in the slaughterhouse game. It's mainly for the screams,' explained Streep, her eyes drifting off as if trying to recall a treasured memory.

'If you see Larry Goodman, tell him I'm coming for his crown!' Streep added, who, like other celebrities such as tequila brand owner Ryan Reynolds, has branched into non-acting pursuits.

Already receiving praise in beef circles, Streep confirmed the tender fillets she produces are down to the

fact they show the cows *Sophie's Choice* on loop.

'Sure, acting is a bit of fun, but it's not what gets me up in the morning. True joy only comes when I'm bringing down a meat cleaver on the neck of an animal. I'm sure if you asked a butcher, they'd say something like, "I wouldn't mind being an actor", which is crazy to me because butchers have the best job in the world,' Streep said, knocking back red liquid from a pint glass which she assured us was 'cranberry juice'.

PAUL MESCAL HASN'T EVEN BEEN IN A MARVEL MOVIE, SO HOW GOOD CAN HE BE?

HOMEGROWN acting sensation Paul Mescal has received nothing but praise for his roles in TV shows, movies and sausage adverts. But can we really take him seriously until he shows up wearing a codpiece and brandishing a laser rifle in the end credits of a superhero movie?

Mescal, who received an Academy Award nomination this year for some indie movie that nine people saw, has yet to truly break out in Hollywood

like his fellow Irish actors, who all knew that portraying a semi-human cartoon character with a nine-syllable name was the key to being considered 'good' at acting.

'Colin Farrell has at least two comic book movies under his belt: *Batman* and *Daredevil*. Barry Keoghan portrayed the first Marvel superhero to say "Howya". You can't move for Gleesons in *Star Wars* and *Harry Potter*,' said our resident film expert, Larry Normal.

'And yet Mescal seems to just want to act in what are described as "good" films. Suit yourself, Paul, but there's only so long an actor will get work as an actor. The key to this business is starring in a two-hour toy commercial.

People won't take you seriously until you're in a scene where you shoot an alien and get covered in slime and say something like, "Boy, I wish I was back in Ballyhaunis!" or something like that.'

Mescal's next role will be in Ridley Scott's *Gladiator* movie, which is a sequel, so that's a start we suppose.

CINEMA

WORLD INFORMS KEANU REEVES HE'S THE ONLY GOOD ONE LEFT, DON'T FUCKING LET US DOWN

AS THE depressingly predictable cavalcade of breaking news stories detailing the various ways in which once beloved celebrities are in fact 'giant shits' continues, the world has once again pleaded with Keanu Reeves to remain a thoroughly nice chap by all accounts.

'You're our only hope,' an open letter to human Labrador puppy Keanu Reeves from eight billion or so people began. 'We love the stories of how you donate loads of money to charity, treat your fans kindly and date a woman your own age', indicating that the bar for qualifying as a 'beloved celebrity' has really nose-dived thanks to the likes of Bill Cosby and Kevin Spacey.

The letter stressed the importance of Reeves' continued decentness, as there is a chronic shortage of genuinely nice famous people.

'Our hearts couldn't take it if you ate kittens or ran a secret underground hobo fighting league, so please just keep popping up in wholesome memes and heartwarming showbiz stories,' begged the world.

UPDATE: The day most people feared has sadly arrived. Keanu Reeves is now *persona non grata* following the publication of a damning picture showing him supplying nuclear arms to North Korea.

LINKEDIN is awash with business advice from underperforming call centre managers and car salesmen, but it doesn't get better than former Waystar Royco CEO Logan Roy for business knowledge.

Here's how to get ahead in business, according to the man himself:

'Fuck off.' This gentle rebuttal of an employee's efforts can help ignite the sort of fire that achieves better results for them, their team and the company.

'If you look at me like that again, I'll rip your eyes out of their sockets with my own hands and have the chef at Eleven Madison Park sauté them so I can eat them, at which point I'll shit them out and put them back in your eye sockets.' Sometimes subtly letting a colleague know you need more from

LOGAN ROY'S PEARLS OF BUSINESS WISDOM

them is the best approach; use this pearl to avoid being too harsh.

'You cretinous flim-flam man, you odious fuck trumpet, you're a contemptible cockatoo, a pendulous prick with the testosterone levels of my wife's book club.' Some of the best business advice doesn't require explaining.

'Is your mother nearby so I can slap her for having the audacity to give birth to the Mona Lisa of disappointments?' Handy line to use when buttering up a client when you need to get a deal over the line.

'The deal? There is no deal. Not anymore, you fucked it.' Best uttered by a Dominos manager when their employee fails to get a customer to order a side with their pizza.

'C'mere and let daddy give you a Glasgow kiss.' If involved in a family business, it's important to keep blood relatives in your good books.

Bill's Political Tips

A businessman doesn't have to donate to your campaign under *his* name, he can do it under his wife's, children's and the family dog's name, too.

Things We've Learned as a Nation

The only thing we hate more than houses not being built is houses being built in our area.

COMEDY

RESEARCH SHOWS JOANNE MCNALLY COULD EASILY MOBILISE ARMY OF TWO MILLION WOMEN, INSTALL MILITARY DICTATORSHIP

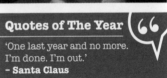

Quotes of The Year

'One last year and no more. I'm done. I'm out.'
– Santa Claus

THE DEPARTMENT of Defence is at its highest level of alert after a report revealed that, such is the reverence and devotion comedian Joanne McNally evokes in the female half of the Irish population, it would be easy for her to mobilise an army of two million women.

A report entitled 'Defence in Ireland', co-authored by security specialists here in Ireland and at the Pentagon, revealed that the obsessive and slavish devotion Irish women have for comedian Joanne McNally makes the extremists joining ISIS look 'flaky' and 'half-arsed'.

'Democracy is fragile at the best of times, but it would only take Joanne to suggest how random it would be for her to take over running the country and a bloody coup would be enacted by some two million gin-cocktail wielding girlos on a session,' one security expert said.

While there is no indication McNally has any designs on installing a prosecco-soaked junta, the report indicates that not even Hitler could dream of inspiring such blind devotion in people.

'Do you have any idea what women armed with high heels in their hands could do if they think they're carrying out the will of their one true goddess Joanne?' concluded a senior Irish military colonel, before frantically ordering barricades for Leinster House.

CLASSICAL MUSIC

'HOW IN THE NAME OF FUCK AM I STILL GETTING AWAY WITH THIS CRAP?'

SMUGLY smirking to himself while casually playing a relatively simple version of 'Silent Night', Dutch violinist and conductor André Rieu looked out at his latest packed venue and wondered to himself how in the name of fuck is he still getting away with this crap.

Bill's Political Tips

Remember, everyone can see your social media likes. Take it from a former liker of 'Big Breasted Milfs' on Facebook.

'Gullible fools,' he muttered to himself, as rows of elderly, highly strung men and women got up off their €120 seats and competitively waltzed in the hopes their hero would give them a glance or a wink – some form of acknowledgement they could mentally take home with them before making love to each other while closing their eyes and imagining it was André himself fiddling them.

'I'll probably get another 20 mill out of this before they cop on that I'm just a mediocre violinist who is more style than substance,' he continued to himself, glancing at his watch

wondering how much bloody longer he has to stand on stage smiling like a buffoon.

'Just look at the want in their eyes,' André thought to himself, content he can still bring in the crowds and take most of the credit for an entire orchestra of professional musicians. 'I could literally stand up here banging a triangle for three hours and they'd still lap it up.'

Now thanking his audience, Rieu calmly raises his violin in the air and bows. 'Half these fuckers will be dead soon; I must tell my agent to pack in as many dates as possible this year.'

CELEBRITIES ━━━━━━━━━━━━━

THE CASE FOR TAYLOR SWIFT DATING ME NEXT

THIS WEEK'S Pop Culture Corner sees *WWN* step away from regular proceedings to let local man Éanna Power make the case for why he should succeed Hollywood actor Joe Alwyn as Taylor's Swift next beau.

Howya Taylor and all that, sound.

Here listen, we'd be fools not to give this a go. Don't be listening to anyone round here, I'm dead on. Don't be listening to Carmel Sheedy, she was only on the one date with me. If she said I suggested riding with the empty packet of Taytos because we had no condoms, she's a liar.

Where was I? Sorry to hear about the fella, but it's best behind ya, out with the old as they say. New day, new dawn, new me, new man, and that's where I come in. Lookit,

I'll stop waffling, listen to me here pouring me feckin' heart out like an eejit. This is what I can offer ya, no messing:

- You'd get some mileage out of me for your songs. Sure, you've been treated poorly by some lads (here's looking at you, Jake Gyllenhaal), but I can guarantee you none of them piss the bed as much as me when I've had one too many. 'Pissed the bed' – sure you can rhyme that with loads of stuff. Albums' worth of material there.
- I'm not judging or nothing, but a quick scan of the room tells me you've dated pretty much everyone else; it's only myself and Tom Macken down the road left, and he's a widower of 80.
- Going lesbian is too obvious. If it's some easy PR you're after, swearing off men and shacking

up with Cara De La Soul, or whatever her name is – that's too obvious. But an out-of-shape Irish lad who's technically between jobs? Now that'll shock people.

- I'm a gentleman in the traditional Irish sense, which is to say I'll hold the door open for you, there'll be no splitting the bill 'cause the mother raised me right, but I'll also be completely unable to handle you texting another lad and will have a full-on meltdown.
- We're about the same height I'd say, so there'd be no adjusting the driver's seat if I was using your car, and we know how much of a pain that can be.

Well, I've said my piece. If you're looking to respond to me directly, the phone is on the blink on account of me not having one, so just email me at powerride69@hotmail.com and we can arrange a date.

TELEVISION

THE CRAZIEST THINGS RTÉ USED ITS BARTER ACCOUNT FOR

REVELATIONS from RTÉ's appearance at the Public Accounts Committee revealed a litany of purchases from what many people have described as a 'slush fund' including €138,000 on Irish rugby tickets and €26,000 on Champions League final tickets among other spending RTÉ says was part of wining and dining clients and brands who spent money on advertising with the station.

Further investigation by *WWN* revealed yet more outrageous largesse bankrolled by RTÉ's barter account, including:

- An item in a ledger just listed as 'prostitutes for Bosco'.
- Copious lines of 'talcum powder' ordered for senior RTÉ figures and talent, which suggests there was a huge nappy rash problem at the broadcaster.
- Spa weekend for Marty Whelan's moustache. Whelan has since clarified that, while he didn't attend, his moustache did.

- €3,965 spent on taxis to Pat Kenny's house just to perform knick knacks on the former RTÉ man's door.
- Helicopter to fly in Kerrygold butter from Kerry to Dáithí Ó Sé's dressing room for his morning toast.
- Absolutely nowhere in the audit was there evidence any money was spent on acting lessons for the *Fair City* cast.
- One member of staff received a one euro bonus every time they correctly added the fada to 'RTÉ' when writing an article on the RTÉ website.
- Paid for clients to spend a night in Queen Elizabeth II's coffin before she was buried.
- Catholic Church was paid €20k per bong in the angelus for use of the church bell copyright, totalling €87 million.
- Claire Byrne's shed was given an all-expenses-paid paid trip to Glastonbury.
- Payments made to a private security firm to help keep Lottie Ryan from sporadically breaking into studio to deliver impromptu entertainment

news during radio programmes were also logged.
- Payments of €250,000 for clients to go on once-in-a-lifetime trip to site of *Titanic* shipwreck at bottom of ocean. Records show clients didn't even have the manners to get in touch and tell them how trip went.
- While purchasing tickets to U2's 2020 concert in Croke Park has made headlines, buried further down in disclosures was the fact RTÉ paid The Coronas not to perform a gig. A rare PR win for the broadcaster.
- Another €50k was spent on head wax for Brian O'Donovan.
- €100,000 to a US cryogenics specialist suggests RTÉ were actively trying to bring back a zombie Gay Byrne to host a number of shows.

Things We've Learned as a Nation

Coleslaw as a culinary delicacy, it shits on caviar and foie gras.

CELEBRITIES

'HE WOULD LOCK ME INTO A BOX AND MAKE ME PERFORM HORRIBLE TASKS WHILE HE WATCHED': SCHOFIELD CO-WORKERS SPEAK OUT

FOLLOWING his dismissal from ITV's *This Morning* show over a feud with co-host Holly Willoughby, more work colleagues have come forward about Phillip Schofield's behaviour behind the scenes.

'He said he'd stick his hand right up my backside,' said former children's TV co-star Gordon the Gopher, recalling one horrifying incident when his usual puppeteer was out sick for an episode. 'Phillip said he would enjoy "doing me" himself and proceeded to shove his fist inside me before mimicking my own voice for an entire 40 minutes while he filmed everything for his own enjoyment. Not one crew member even stopped him.'

Similarly, a fellow *Cube* staff member detailed horrific psychological mind games carried out by the 61-year-old where she was forced to wear a strange helmet before being shoved into a box to perform an array of mundane tasks.

'He liked to make me pick up balls as he watched through Perspex glass, taunting me, saying that I'll never be better than a cube,' the staff member told *WWN*. 'He liked to constantly compare my intelligence to the inanimate object; it seemed to give him pleasure.'

Meanwhile, as the string of revelations slowly emerges, it has been reported that UK TV viewers have been behind a 5000% increase in the number of people googling the words 'Schofield', 'grooming', 'injunction' and 'super' over the past couple of months.

CINEMA

BLACKBIRD ROBBED AT BAFTAS

FANS of the number one Irish blockbuster film of the century have called for a total boycott of the BAFTAs after their favourite film didn't even secure one single nomination or award, sending shockwaves through the film industry.

Despite a good result for inferior Irish movies such as *The Banshees of Inisherin*, the Michael Flatley masterpiece *Blackbird* went unmentioned at the prestigious awards ceremony, sparking conspiracy theories that if nominated, *Blackbird* would have only overshadowed the James Bond franchise and showed the Brits up on home soil.

'Begorrah, they're obviously shaking in their brógs it was that good,' movie expert MF36543@ hotmail.com told *WWN* during a lengthy email correspondence. 'To be sure, to be sure, *Blackbird* is one of the most iconic movies made in our time, and the lead actor delivered one of the finest performances the world has ever seen.'

Similarly, hundreds of more movie critics echoed this sentiment, with MF36578@hotmail.com stating that Michael Flatley should have won every single category last night and called on BAFTA judges to reconsider their voting system for future *Blackbird* movies that may be produced down the line.

'All I keep hearing from just about everybody I meet is "I wish there were more *Blackbird* movies I could watch"' and "Michael Flatley is so sexy for his age and has never lost it",' another movie critic at the email address MF36876@hotmail.com confirmed.

Unavailable for comment, the ever-modest Michael Flatley remained stoically silent on the whole fiasco.

UPDATE: A 'Justice for Blackbird' protest has seen several petrol bombs hurled through the windows of various BAFTA voters.

Quotes of The Year ❝

'We would have won the World Cup if only for [insert insane reason here].'
- Irish sports fan

CRIME

INCREDIBLE! MAN COMMITTING CRIME PREDICTED HE'D BE ARRESTED FOR COMMITTING CRIME

IN WHAT has been described as sorcery by some followers, a British man who was committing crimes in Romania has somehow predicted on multiple occasions that he would be arrested for committing those crimes, sparking theories that he was right about himself all along.

Andrew Tate, a former kickboxer turned full-time asshole, was arrested by Romanian authorities over human trafficking, rape, and various other crimes after giving away his location during a callout video to a teenage climate change activist after she hurt his feelings on Twitter.

'Andrew said this would happen and he was right,' thousands of his followers quickly pointed out, seemingly astounded at his stunning ability to predict his own demise. 'This is the Matrix man, they've got him, just like he said they would,' the followers added, like a point was made somewhere.

Tate, who recently shot to fame by bombarding social networks with paid-for posts and multi-level marketing schemes, acquired

the majority of his wealth by collaborating with the Russian Mafia in Eastern Bloc countries, creating dodgy casinos and gambling firms, along with running online 'hustler' courses for insecure young men who seem to be regularly turned down by members of the opposite sex.

'Yeah, yeah, he openly admits to all of this so we don't see what your point is,' his dedicated fans retorted when presented with the facts, still not quite putting two and two together. 'Andrew called it months ago, man, he knew they'd do this, he knew they'd silence him in the end for committing a litany of heinous crimes,' they continued, some slowly realising they may have been hoodwinked, but in denial all the same.

Meanwhile, Greta Thunberg has been asked to now focus her attention on a growing number of questionable men returning to Twitter under Elon Musk's amnesty. She refused, stating that the world doesn't have that much time left to deal with the amount of dickheads out there.

HERE'S AN UNFLATTERING PHOTO OF A CELEBRITY WE'VE CHOSEN TO GOAD YOU INTO SHITTING ON

THAT actor from that thing you watched 30 years ago looks totally unrecognisable today, and just look at this picture we illegally snapped of her in a vulnerable position.

Stuck for money to pay our high-end paparazzi this week, we sent our intern, Dave from accounts, down the road to try to snap a picture of someone, anyone of vague interest in a bid to get you all piling into the comments section to say your piece.

Comments like 'She's really let herself go', 'What happened to her face?' and 'She's obviously depressed' are all fair game here, so please let your poisonous little fingers do their thing while we reap the benefits of paid advertising banners selling you things you don't need under the guise of 'news and entertainment'.

Phrases from our report like 'Doesn't she look great?' and 'You go, girl' goad you into witty putdowns via anonymous Twitter handles that shame this once-beloved actor into oblivion in the hopes it fills the never-ending void in your scurrilous heart.

Join us for tomorrow's article on how said celebrity takes trolls to task.

BREAKING

NAKED MARES, COCAINE, EMPTY BOTTLES OF NITROUS OXIDE: INSIDE JENNY THE DONKEY'S HOTEL ROOM AT OSCARS AFTER PARTY

STAFF at the Chateau Marmont hotel in LA have begun a massive clean-up operation after a late-night sex- and drugs-fuelled party took place in *The Banshees of Inisherin* star Jenny the Donkey's hotel room, *WWN* reports.

Animal control officers were seen leading out 'buckled mares' barely able to walk from the hotel, along with countless empty bottles of nitrous oxide and various other drug and drink paraphernalia.

'The last time I saw a strap-on and sex swing in here was in Johnny Depp's heyday,' stated night porter Miguel Iglesias, who spent the night going up and down with trays of drinks and 'special requests' for the guests. 'Some of those mares couldn't have been more than four years old,' he added. 'I had to call animal welfare when the hot tub cracked, sending water gushing into the rooms below.'

The disgraced donkey was led out of the premises around 7 a.m. with white powder visibly caked to its nostrils, but not before bucking several times and assaulting security and LAPD officers. Jenny's agent has since denied reports the star was found with one kilo of ketamine in her possession.

> ## 'Some of those mares couldn't have been more than four years old'

'I agree that this kind of carry on doesn't bode well for Irish stereotypes,' *Banshees* co-star Brendan Gleeson later commented on the incident, 'but if anyone finds my phone in the room, please let me know.'

RADIO

HOW ABOUT YOU PLAY SOME MUSIC AND SHUT THE FUCK UP, RADIO DJS FINALLY TOLD

SICK to its core of the relentless, nonsensical jibber-jabber, the Irish nation made a joint statement this week urging radio DJs to just give it a fucking rest for at least one day and play some God-given decent music, *WWN* has learned.

Unsure at what point radio DJs formed the delusion that listeners want to know about their lives, the nation quickly nipped the chatter in the bud and gave it to them straight.

'We don't care about how you deal with stress, what you had for lunch, what famous name you're dropping; we just want to hear some sick tunes,' a joint statement

> **'We don't care about how you deal with stress, what you had for lunch, what famous name you're dropping'**

from Ireland read, officially signed by President Michael D. Higgins to give it more value.

'Shut. The. Fuck. Up.' the statement added. 'There's enough time wasted on ads and competitions, phone-ins and news without having to listen to you spare pricks prattling on about how you store your ketchup. Give it up to fuck.'

Responding to the five million-signature-strong statement, a collection of upset radio DJs called on the nation to go listen to some AI-run radio stations, if they're that painful to listen to, with the nation quickly replying, 'Oh, don't worry, we will.'

CELEBRITIES

'I HAVE TWO MICKIES,' DAVID HAYE REVEALS

AFTER updating his throuple following the recent departure of Una Healy, former professional boxer and all-round lad David Haye has revealed he actually has two mickies, *WWN Entertainment Buzz* can reveal.

'Peeing can be a disaster, but apart from that they work pretty well,' said the 42-year-old during an interview with *WWN*. 'They also make really cool slapping noises when I swing my hips from side to side and, obviously, I'm great in bed.'

Mr Haye went on to state that although one micky is shorter than the other, he insisted it's not the size that matters, but how you use it.

'My full-time girl Sian obviously gets to keep the longer one, so any new squeeze makes do with the DeVito – that's what I call him, Danny DeVito,' Haye added, now fixing himself as he sat in his chair. 'Excuse me, sometimes I have to peel my nut sacks off my legs, it's quite crowded down there.'

David took to his Instagram to show off the new woman in his life, Mica Jova, who is in no way doing this for the attention.

'God no, I just love being the third wheel in a throuple and little DeVito is all I need to be satisfied, that and the several thousand followers I'm going to get out of all of this,' Mica concluded.

BREAKING NEWS

BELOVED ACTOR WE'RE NOT NAMING UNTIL YOU CLICK HAS DIED

GOT YOU! We knew you'd click. Nothing like a celebrity death to get you buckos in the door.

Absolutely, we could have mentioned who it was in the headline, but then we wouldn't get this vital pageview on our stats. It's hard times for online publishers these days, so we're having to coax you in with teasing headlines that spark interest. Sorry about that.

Sure, this dead celebrity may not be well-known and actually just the bassist in a lesser-known alternative band from the 1970s, but we have to eat too.

Hopefully all the dozen or so pops-ups you had to click to get here weren't too annoying now that you realise you've been duped into reading an article about someone you never even heard of. So far, you've wasted at least 30 seconds, which is about our average dwell time, so feel free to fuck off back to your precious social network feed or wherever you found this link.

Still here? Feel free to look around. Click a banner ad and make us two cents. Refresh this page and give us another page view. Please, we're fucking desperate.

Predictions for 2024

Someone will have an accident at work that actually was their fault.

BREAKING ━━━━━━━━━━━━━━━━━━━━━━━━━━━━━━━━

TRUMP DEMANDS TO BE TRIED BY JUDGE JUDY

IN THE first of many attempts to pervert the course of justice on the day of his arraignment, Donald Trump has instructed his lawyers to demand the former US president be tried by a real judge like Judge Judy.

'She's the best; she's tough but fair. The radical left won't like it, but I've always felt she judges Judily, she judges fairly, everyone says it,' offered Trump.

'Maybe she will treat me right because we are both TV stars, but

maybe she won't, which is OK because my supporters only need to take one look at her surname, Sheindlin – very suspect, very "Soros" don't you think? And before you criticise, it's not antisemitic if you don't say the quiet part out loud,' Trump added.

Attempting to circumvent the sort of processes and justice an ordinary citizen would be subject to had they allegedly committed the crimes he is accused of, Trump is seeking a number of additional concessions, including:

- That the DA reconsider the whole 'must answer for crimes' thing.
- He be allowed to address the court in ALL CAPS.

- Permission to replace his defence counsel with an in-court Fox News studio.
- That the 40,000 cameras and reporters outside the court interviewing the handful of Trump supporters who were bothered to show up continue to do so.
- A moment of someone's time so they can explain what 'indictment', 'arraignment' and 'guilty' mean.
- A guarantee that no one will be allowed bring up in court the fact that Stormy Daniels said he has a tiny dick.
- He be allowed to finish every answer with the live location of District Attorney Alvin Bragg's wife and children, just in case any lunatics out there are interested.

SOCIAL MEDIA

SHIV ROY ANNOUNCED AS NEW TWITTER CEO

UPDATE: Shiv Roy, former Waystar Royco executive, confirmed to succeed Elon Musk as Twitter CEO.

Pipping Elizabeth Holmes and Ed Norton's girlfriend from *American History X* to the post, the 35-year-old scion of the Roy media empire was a surprise choice, but she will take charge in under six weeks.

'I'm stepping down to spend more time on my true business passion, which is exploding rockets and cars, and let's not forget killing monkeys with brain chips,' Musk said in his Twitter statement announcing Roy's appointment.

'Making a woman clean up my mess is very on brand, isn't it?' added Musk, who was just happy to find the woman who will be blamed for all the monumentally shortsighted and idiotic policy decisions he has made since spending $44 billion on the social media company.

Ardent fans of Musk were said to be upset at the billionaire giving in to the woke brain disease by appointing a woman, who, in Roy's case, has previously worked for Democratic politicians in Washington, including the hard-left, woke, Antifa-loving Gil Eavis, who makes Bernie Sanders look like Henry Ford.

However, those fears were allayed when it was pointed out Waystar Royco had a high-profile scandal involving the rape and sexual assault of staff on their cruise ships, which resulted in several deaths. It is also the parent company of right-wing cable network ATN, which is even a little too openly white supremacist for Tucker Carlson.

In the wake of the announcement, Roy's brother Roman Roy tweeted '#GirlBoss'.

UPDATE: Elon Musk has been forced to deny sending a female staff member blocks of his frozen blood.

Dictionary Additions of 2024

'Beergaining': the pleading that takes place in a supermarket when you try to buy alcohol at 10:01 p.m.

Quotes of The Year

'Fuck me, they really have forgotten everything, haven't they?'
– Bertie Aherne

WHAT BARRY KEOGHAN'S MET GALA OUTFIT MEANS FOR THIS YEAR'S COMMUNION SUIT TRENDS

WHILE the celebrity and fashion world came together at the Met Gala in New York, at home in Ireland the country's communion suit and dress makers drowned in their own tears knowing that a fresh wave of outlandish and unrealistic demands was about to come crashing down on them.

'They all want "The Keoghan" now after seeing Barry do his thing on the red carpet. Where do these parents think I'm going to find metres and metres of navy and black Burberry fabric-roll ends at such short notice?' a frantic June O'Brien, proprietor of Child Brides Communion Emporium, told *WWN*.

It is unusual for the Met Gala to directly influence communion season, as it normally falls to the convention-defying, show-stopping outfits on display during Irish communion season to influence the Met Gala.

'It's not the kids, it's the mams I blame. They see a bit of the Met Gala on Instagram and they're straight down to me with the demands. One mam wants her son in a giant cat suit like Jared Leto, and do you think she'd accept a "no"?' added O'Brien, who believes the communion catwalks this year will be dominated by Met Gala-influenced looks.

A close second behind Keoghan's look in terms of demands by Irish parents is the 'Daddy Satan on his day off' red and black outfit donned by Pedro Pascal, about which local priests have already issued warnings. However, some parents have defended following these trends.

'If my little Jamie wants to be sprayed with silver body paint and wear a bejewelled mask like Lil Nas X then that's what he's getting. I'll never hear the end of it if I put him in a boring blazer and slacks, and all his friends outshining him because they're Burberry'd up t'fuck,' offered one concerned parent.

Elsewhere, a Tipperary farmer on holiday in New York has sparked a resurgence in the bootcut jeans with brown shoes trend after mistakenly finding himself on the red carpet at the Met Gala.

CELEBRITIES

UNA HEALY FANS ALL SAY THE SAME THING AS SHE SPINS SILK CHRYSALIS, ATTACHES SELF TO TREE

FANS of Una Healy all said the same thing after she stripped to her essentials, squatted down, and started weaving strings of silk from her nether regions into a beautiful chrysalis before attaching herself to a large tree in County Tipperary.

The six-foot cocoon solidified onto the tree like cement as images appeared on Una's Instagram channel, sparking rumours that the former Saturdays star may undergo metamorphosis and become an even more beautiful butter-person ahead of summer.

Una's friends and fans all went wild for her stunning chrysalis snaps.

'Good on you, Una, fair play. I'm glad someone finally did it,' said one fan showing their support for the Tipperary native's bravery in opting to transform into a winged human– Rhopalocera hybrid capable of flight.

'What the actual fuck is going on here, seriously?' posted several other fans, all saying the same thing as our headline suggested.

'Whatever she morphs into, I know for a fact she will still

> **'Whatever she morphs into, I know for a fact she will still be gorgeous'**

be gorgeous, and she should be respected for that despite this tough and painful mutation,' one caterpillar commented, eating a leaf of cabbage.

It is unclear how long Una will remain attached to the Tipperary tree before eclosion, and whether she will emerge with a tubular sucking organ, known as a proboscis, allowing her to extract sweet nectar from the flowers she will then feed upon.

'Oh boy, a proboscis sure sounds like a lot of fun,' David Haye later commented on the post.

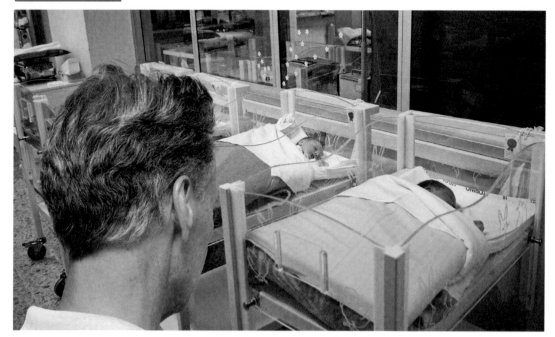

CORONATION STREET PRODUCER SCOUTS MANCHESTER MATERNITY WARD FOR NEXT LIFE-LONG ACTOR

THERE was a buzz in a Manchester hospital this afternoon as *Coronation Street* producer Damien Harte began searching for the next child actor to fulfil a life-long role working at the now 62-year-old programme, *WWN* has learned.

With parents watching on from the side, Harte went from bed to bed checking the babies for potential talent, measuring facial features, and asking them to soil themselves on cue in a process he was now all too familiar with over his 43-year career.

'I'm looking for the next David Platt,' Harte explained, shortlisting the remaining babies by requesting all the red-haired ones be removed. 'Don't get me wrong, Chesney was great, but gingers are notoriously difficult to work with and have a bit of a temper.'

With the shortlist now down to four potentials, a couple of actors were brought into gauge how the future young star will perform around their new on-screen parents while they argued over infidelity.

'Punch her, Joe, then push her to the ground,' he shouted at the actors, staring intently at the babies' reactions, homing in on the baby making the most horrid wailing noise. 'Yes, yes, brilliant timing here; this little one senses the anxiety in the room and is reacting exactly like we want it to – like it's absolutely terrified to bits. Brilliant work.'

'We'll take this one!' he said as he was treated to a large round of applause from parents and hospital

> **'Chesney was great, but gingers are notoriously difficult to work with and have a bit of a temper'**

staff, while lifting the child in the air like that scene from *The Lion King*. 'A new *Coronation Street* star is born!'

Signing over their first born in exchange for a nice steady weekly wage, lucky parents Geraldine and Patrick Hogan embraced each other at the news.

'I can't believe Harriot is going to be in *Coronation Street* for life,' her mother stated, now waving her child goodbye for the last time. 'We can't wait to watch you growing up on our favourite show every weekday at half seven and see all the God-awful scenarios you'll have to endure – just have fun with it, darling. Good luck!'

Predictions for 2024

Nyan cat will die, aged 13. To the sky you go, kitty.

w w news

Waterford Whispers News

LIFESTYLE

CRIME

ELDERLY MAN CAUGHT WITH SPLIFF ASKS JUDGE TO TREAT HIM LIKE SEX OFFENDER

AN ELDERLY man, who was just handed a custodial prison sentence for being found in possession of cannabis he used to cope with chronic pain, has pleaded with the District Court to instead treat him like a sex offender in the hopes of a more lenient punishment.

'Can't we just pretend I'm after downloading the most repugnant and

'Can't we just pretend I'm after downloading the most repugnant and disgusting images you've ever seen?'

disgusting images you've ever seen? That way it's a suspended sentence, and I can head home today without being thrown in prison and given a criminal record,' said now-convicted criminal Sean Crattigan after hearing the sentence handed down by Judge John Folan.

'Seriously, I'm talking the most depraved imagery imaginable. You know, the type that would have you run out of town by an angry mob,' added Crattigan, seemingly trying to exploit an unconfirmed legal loophole in sentencing, which sees the possession of such images as 'a bit of harmless craic' within the Irish judicial system.

Replying to the defendant, Judge Folan denied the request, citing the seriousness of cannabis possession and pointing out the fact that even if he was to be treated as a nonce, he didn't call on a priest or GAA manager to stand for him as a character witness 'like all good perverts would do'.

Crattigan was handed a three-month prison sentence by the judge who then called on court reporters to take a picture of the criminal and publish it in local and national newspapers for everyone to see.

FOR THE LOVE OF CHRIST, SEAN

FRIENDS of Dublin man Sean O'Coughlain sighed in exasperation today when the 25-year-old showed up to meet them in the pub wearing one of those cross-body bum bag things that are apparently all the rage these days.

'Sean just … just no, OK? Just fucking no,' exclaimed Mark Whelan, who stomached O'Coughlain's 'year of the mullet' in 2019 but has reached absolute breaking point with this nonsense.

'Yeah, Sean, do you ever think of the rest of us when you do these things? You're not "the lad with the stupid bag thing". We're all "the lads with the lad with the stupid bag thing",' added Eddie Harper, trying to reason with O'Coughlain to just use his pockets like everyone else.

Nevertheless, O'Coughlain was adamant that his new cross-body bum bag thing, the real name of which escaped him at that moment, was an essential part of his wardrobe these days and that 'if they tried one, they'd agree it was cool'.

'You can keep your phone in it, your Leap card … your phone and your Leap card. It's not a purse and it's not a bum bag from the nineties, it's something new and cool and it's part of me now,' he explained, minutes before his pals erupted in derision when he told them how much he paid for the fucking thing.

DAD STILL SENDING FARMVILLE REQUESTS

DESPITE it being over a decade since it was a thing, local Farmville diehard Mark Jenkins is still sending family members and friends Farmville requests like it's 2010, *WWN* reports.

'He poked me the other day; I didn't even know Facebook still had that feature,' daughter Jessica opened up. 'Apparently he asked me to send him a bag of fertilizer for his farm and I didn't see the notification – little does he know I blocked him ages ago.'

Jenkins admits he hasn't quite moved on from the glory days of Facebook, but he is very proud of how his farm turned out.

'If I had this farm back in 2010, everyone would be asking me for gifts,' said the 58-year-old, taking a break from Farmville to play some Zynga Poker instead.

'You know Zuckerberg was on to something back then, when Facebook was all about community and friendship and socialising. Alas, now it's all arguments and division, whether you're on the right or on the left – it's all gone to shite, so excuse me if I want to hold on to something special that involves community spirit,' he concluded, before verbally fucking a fellow Zynga Poker player out of it for getting a full house on the flop.

RELIGION

'DID YOU JUST ASSUME MY RELIGION?' CALLS TO FINE PEOPLE WHO BLESS SNEEZING

DO YOU bless people after they sneeze? Well, you could soon receive a €500 fine for a first offense and a €1,000 fine thereafter if the left-wing woke nutjobs that we just made up for the purpose of this poorly orchestrated article get their demented way.

Assuming a person's religion is the latest trend we've managed to concoct in the hopes you just share this headline without bothering to read it, fuelling mass debate online about how Christianity is the latest thing being cancelled and erased by the left-wing mainstream media industrial complex, only to be replaced with Islamic grooming gangs hell-bent on infiltrating every blonde, white girl on this once pure, pure island of ours.

'People who force their beliefs on other people by blessing their sneezes should be fined; it's so offensive to assume I even have a religion,' is a nice handy quote we'll say is from a transgender atheist, for maximum effect.

We could be covering other news but our parent company in the UK thinks this shit-stirring helps distract people from growing inequality, and we couldn't agree more.

'You can't assume people's faith like that, not in today's world,' is another anonymous quote we'll slot into the article's subheading, which should be sufficient to generate enough

> ## 'People who force their beliefs on other people by blessing their sneezes should be fined'

apoplexy to get people to lose their tiny little minds and share the article.

To help fund the continued destruction of civil society as we know it by the secret woke police, you can send cash to the *WWN* headquarters.

EXCLUSIVE

'I LISTEN BACK TO MY OWN VOICE NOTES BECAUSE I'M THAT HILARIOUS'

LOCAL woman Martina Phelan admits to not only spending countless hours recording voice notes to friends, but even more time listening to them as she's that hilarious, *WWN* reports.

'I like to speed up my friend's voice notes and, to be honest, I sometimes scrub through them altogether as I can't really be arsed listening to what they're saying – am I terrible?' Martina said, analysing her

own logic, now laughing at her gas impression of her boss that she sent to a work colleague who must be in absolute hysterics listening to it right now, if not already in hospital with split sides.

Phelan also admits to making her partner listen to her gas voice notes and will grab the remote control and pause whatever silly sport he has on the TV if she feels he's not fully committed to her ramblings.

'He's probably asking himself what kind of mad bitch he's going out with – what am I like?' Phelan went on, now re-recording a voice note as the last one she made didn't emphasise

Quotes of The Year

'Ah, it's a bit dear, but fuck it, it's not like I'm paying for it.'
– John Delaney

her Joanne McNally-type accent enough, a party piece she loves to do for the girls.

'She's fucking relentless and if you don't pay attention to her stupid voice notes she'll literally flay you with a Stanley blade,' terrified long-time friend Lacey Stevens stated, admitting she is unable to ignore Phelan's barrage of late-evening conversations with herself for fear of her life. 'I'm actually moving away soon and changing my name by deed poll so hopefully I'll get some respite soon.'

Council Notices

Parts of Roscommon are currently on a Boyle notice until further notified.

MOTORING

A GROUNDBREAKING new report into slow punctures has found it's better to keep pumping your faulty car tyre than actually going to the bother of fixing it.

The study found that the tedious chore of finding a garage that doesn't charge you a euro for compressed air and then getting out in the lashing rain to pump the bastard is more beneficial to you and your family's safety than coughing up 10 quid.

'It's way more fun driving with a possible blowout risk,' the study found. 'The potential accident would be worth it in the long run as driving these days is way too uneventful. It's best to have a challenge, like avoiding an oncoming truck, with your kids in the back of your car, when the tyre explodes sending you swerving under the truck's front axles, mincing everyone in the car for the fire brigade to scrape up.'

Previously, the researchers of the study also found that leaving your petrol constantly in the red will

BETTER TO KEEP PUMPING UP CAR TYRE THAN REPAIRING IT, STUDY FINDS

ensure you never run out of fuel in the middle of a roundabout during

rush hour, forcing everyone else to be late for work.

DUBLIN GIRL WAS TOLD SUCCULENT PLANTS WERE IMPOSSIBLE TO KILL, BUT HERE WE ARE

SUCCULENT plants such as cacti and aloe have evolved over millennia to survive the harshest, most arid conditions this earth has to offer. Despite this, they have yet to evolve enough to survive the apartment of

Dublin native Erin O'Hanlon, who has managed to kill off her entire collection in one year.

'They said these things just need a little water and, like, some sunlight? But I watered them at Christmas and

they can kinda get a bit of sunlight where they are, and now they're all gross and brown and dead and stuff?' said 23-year-old O'Hanlon, looking at the desiccated plants that litter the top of her wardrobe.

'I read you can kill them through over-watering and I can promise you that didn't happen. I bought them, took a selfie with them, called them my "new spike babies lol" and then left them on the press there for 12 months and now they're dead?'

O'Hanlon's ability to murder her plants has amazed co-workers, many of whom have had succulent plants on their desks for nearly a decade.

'We went into lockdown and worked from home for three years. and when I came back the cactus on my desk was still in full health,' said one amazed co-worker. 'Erin could kill a pet rock.'

Current theories about how O'Hanlon managed the seemingly impossible include fumigating the plant with a constant fog of vape or 'talking so much shite that the damn thing committed suicide'.

SOCIAL MEDIA

INTERVENTION STAGED FOR MATE WHO KEEPS SENDING GRAPHIC WHATSAPP VIDEOS

'FOR fuck's sake, John, no one wants to see a video of someone getting minced by a metro train at two o'clock in the morning, it's just not right,' Mark Rice told his long-time friend John Clear during a special sitting of the WhatsApp group 'The Lads' in Regan's Bar, Waterford.

'Yeah, John, I was sitting watching Cirque du Soleil with the wife and kids when I opened that Mexican drug cartel video of them flaying

Dictionary Additions of 2024

'Ahno': the sound someone makes when they see on Twitter that a celebrity they like has died.

some guy on a chair,' added Derry Ryan, another participant of The Lads group. 'My five-year-old, who was sitting on my lap at the time, is still haunted by that brief glimpse of the image.'

John Clear nodded as, one-by-one, his friends recounted horrific videos he had sent in unsolicited messages, videos that unknowingly downloaded onto one mate's camera roll.

'Jane left me over the bestiality porn you sent when we were looking at old holiday snaps with her folks on the phone,' an emotional David Tobin chimed in. 'You try and explain how that was in my Amsterdam pics, John, you sick fuck.'

Agreeing to 'tone it down a bit from now on', the 43-year-old promised the

Predictions for 2024

The NCT will offer you a test in 2027.

group of 'pussies' that in future he will think before sending images or videos of a graphic nature.

'It's only a bit of craic, lads, but I'll definitely take everything you said into consideration,' he concluded, just as multiple notifications pinged those in attendance.

'Fucking hell, John, how did you even send that while we were talking?' everyone replied in horror, as the sound of an orgasming woman echoed loudly around the busy pub.

SOCIALISING

WOMAN SOMEHOW FOUND HERSELF IN POSITION OF ORGANISING HEN FOR OLD SCHOOL FRIEND SHE HASN'T SEEN IN 10 YEARS

DECLARED by observers to be the 'ultimate nightmare' and a horror show that outdoes the new *Evil Dead* movie, local woman Shannon Scannon has stumbled her way into organising a hen for an old school friend she's had next to no dealings with in the last ten years.

The dangers to her jaw and cheeks from sustained pretend smiling and faking excitement at a wedding you didn't think you'd get an invite to, let alone undertaking hen-organising duties, could see Scannon need corrective surgery.

'A stripper? Yeah OK, sounds good,' replied Scannon to a group of complete strangers and bride-to-be Maura Cowlan's latest text about the hen party.

Promoted to hen-organising duties due to Clare being pregnant, Julie doing her final project for her masters and Shona C., Rachel, Kelly, Maria, Shona B., Martina and Laura all living in Australia, Scannon admitted she brought this on herself.

'If I'd just had the courage to unfollow her on Instagram eight years ago, block her number, move to

another country and change identity, none of this would be happening,' offered Scannon.

'Cool, cool, cool, no problem,' Scannon texted, after Cowlan informed her of having a five-day hen in Vegas, which should only come to €2,500 all-in.

TECHNOLOGY

OWNERS OF NEW AIR FRYER DRIVE GEORGE FOREMAN MACHINE TO FOREST, LEAVE IT THERE

THE Irish Society for the Prevention of Cruelty to Kitchen Gadgets has issued a plea for cooking enthusiasts around the country to consider their existing gizmos before thinking about purchasing an air fryer, amid heartbreaking tales of abandoned panini grills and NutriBullets.

'This is a brilliant little George Foreman grill that we found on the side of the road earlier this week,' said a spokesperson for the ISPCKG, holding a two-year-old lean, mean, grillin' machine.

'Someone had driven it out to the woods and just left it there. And this is not an isolated incident – more and more, people are seeing these fancy new air fryers on Instagram and heading out to get one without considering if they have the time or space for it in their kitchen. When that happens, something has to go, such as this once-beloved grill.'

Urging people that a kitchen doohickie is for life, not just the weeks after you come home drunk and sit watching the shopping channel after 1 a.m., the ISPCKG projected a bleak future for the abandoned whatchamacallums.

'We're trying to find suitable homes for all these slap-chops and slow cookers, but the cold, hard truth of the matter is that most will be destroyed,' we were told.

'So please, think about things before you buy an air fryer. Will you ever use

> **'We're trying to find suitable homes for all these slap-chops and slow cookers, but the cold, hard truth of the matter is that most will be destroyed'**

it? Do you really want your food to be dryer and not that nice? Isn't the press above the sink already rammed full of half-washed black machines with cables everywhere?'

If you have read this article and would still like to buy an air fryer, use the code BUYTHINGS for 10% off your purchase.

GETTING BOTOX: THE PROS AND CONS

PRO: The lack of facial expressions will make it harder for the police to tell if you're lying.
CON: If you sneeze mid-injection your face will be stuck like that.

PRO: Your face will no longer resemble the dry, crease-ridden hide of an elephant's testicle.
CON: No matter how much you protest, your local beauty therapist will not accept Monopoly money as payment.

PRO: You'll finally be happy and accept yourself.
CON: LOL, as if! You'll still be your miserable self-loathing self.

PRO: If it's good enough for Michael D. Higgins, it's good enough for you.
CON: If no one notices you've got it, does that mean it's working or not?

PRO: Botox is produced in Mayo, so technically you're supporting the local economy.
CON: You're not sure if the transition year work experience kid should be the one administering this to you.

PRO: It's not permanent, unlike your lack of self-esteem.
CON: The botulinum toxin can spread beyond the treatment area, causing botulism-like symptoms such as breathing problems, trouble swallowing, muscle weakness and slurred speech. No worse than a night out on the drink, in fairness.

PRO: You'll be the primary source of local gossip in your town for at least a month.

LIFE COACH'S LIFE A FUCKING MESS

ADMITTING to initially studying psychology in the hopes of one day trying to decipher his own galaxy of issues, life coach Terry Dalton defiantly trooped on with his career choice regardless, hoping none of his clients ever realise what an absolute fuck-up he really is.

'Christ, if they ever found out the insane shite I get up to, they'd have me committed,' the five-time married 34-year-old explained. 'The alcoholism, the drugs, the three hookers I hired on Monday night to suck me off while watching *Love Island* – sure, you can't help people if you're not fucked up yourself.'

Dalton, who changed his name by Deed Poll in 2009 due to a litany of fraud allegations, said there is nothing more rewarding than helping other people deal with their issues, something he has a huge problem with himself.

'Ran the Range Rover into a group of cyclists while drunk on Sunday,' Dalton recalls. 'Apparently the news said no one was hurt in the hit and run, so someone's looking down on me at least.'

With an impressive catalogue of Instagram influencer clients who think they're celebrities on his books, Dalton counts his blessings every day and said he's not really in it for the money anymore, it's all about the people.

'One of my clients told the *Irish Daily Mail* last week that she's never felt better since I started coaching her. It's those little things that make it all worthwhile,' he added. 'Hopefully she doesn't find out those vitamins are actually speed tabs, but lookit, we'll take it one day at a time.'

SEX

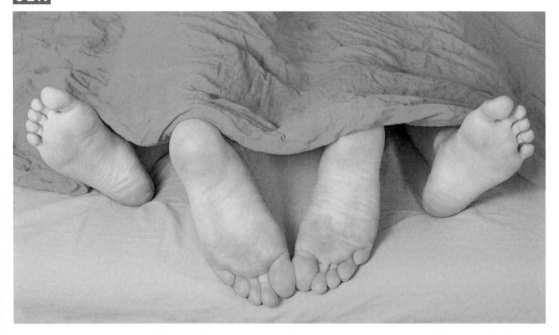

YOUNG PEOPLE ASKED WHAT'S WRONG WITH JUST NORMAL RIDING?

A NEW sex education module being trialled in some schools is hoping to wean teenagers away from today's world of threesomes and butt play and God knows what else, and back to a more traditional sexual landscape with normal, old-fashioned sex.

'Somewhere along the way, the youth of today got it in their heads that sex was supposed to be, if you can believe

> **'We realise that we can't stop them from having sex – that ship has sailed'**

it, fun and exciting,' said Sr Mary Phillip Joseph, the nun heading up the new initiative.

'We realise that we can't stop them from having sex – that ship has sailed – but we're hoping they can perhaps learn how these things used to happen, where nobody really enjoyed it and there was a nice cloud of shame and sin hanging over the whole thing.'

The programme, which so far has only been adopted by the strictest of Catholic schools, encourages the following:

- A return to classic, 'old-school' heavy-petting while fully clothed and standing, as opposed to

Predictions for 2024

The world begins to suspect there's something not quite right about this Trump lad.

anything with a degree of comfort and intimacy.
- If you must use contraception, then be sure to pray for forgiveness afterwards.
- The only 'threesome' you should be having is with the Lord. 'Jesus is always with you, so technically all sex is an orgy,' Sr Mary Phillip Joseph told us.

The module contains no guidelines for gay teenagers in need of sex advice, as they can 'figure it out themselves if they insist on being that way'.

Quotes of The Year 66

'Why is it so bloody hot down here?'
- **Rolf Harris**

THE IRISH LANDLORD LEAGUE PRESENTS
EVICTION
fest
APRIL 1ST - EVERYWHERE - IRELAND
Masked Men
The Gardaí
The Black Eyed Tenants
On The Streets
30-Day Notice - HAP Me Bollocks
What Deposit - Rent Increases - Toothless RTB
Emergency Accommodation - Brother Moving In
Special Guests: Landlord TDs
And many more!
TICKETS START FROM €3,000pm
EMAIL DARRAGH.OBRIEN@OIREACHTAS.IE FOR MORE INFO
SPONSORED BY IRES REIT

SOCIALISING

WOMAN COULDN'T DRINK FROM WATER BOTTLE ANY LOUDER IF SHE TRIED

WHETHER it's in the gym, on the bus or at the office, Waterford woman Sheila Ross is constantly taking slurps from her water bottle that are as loud as a cow pissing on a flat stone, *WWN* can report.

Ross, 35, 'genuinely could not drink any louder if her life depended on it' according to her co-workers, who have to sit through the gurgling, slushing noises at a rate of one slurp every 90 seconds or so.

To make matters worse, the Waterford woman has purchased a water bottle that makes the noise of someone taking a bong rip, as opposed to her pouring water into a glass and drinking it quietly.

'What's wrong with glasses, eh? Why did we have to do away with glasses and introduce bottles that sound like a two-stroke engine ticking over?' sighed one of Ross' long-suffering co-workers.

'The next time I'm giving an important presentation and all anyone can hear is Sheila making more noise than the Poulaphouca generator, it will be the first time it could be said that drinking water could be bad for your health.'

Ross was unavailable for comment, as she was continuously slurping water

> **'Why did we have to do away with glasses and introduce bottles that sound like a two-stroke engine ticking over?'**

as if she was in imminent danger of dying from dehydration.

Bill's Political Tips

Keep all your rental properties off the Dáil Register of Members' Interests, that way gullible constituents will think you're one of them.

Dictionary Additions of 2024

'Roadworks roulette': a fun motorist game that commuters are forced to play when choosing the quickest route to work only to be delayed by unannounced roadworks.

WWN LIFE HACK

FORGET TURKEY, THIS TIPP-EX HACK WILL SAVE YOU THOUSANDS ON DENTAL WORK

WITH thousands of people flying abroad to avail of cheaper dental work, *WWN Life Hacks* is back again with some tips to cut even more costs from your life with simple hacks that may or may not also cut your lifespan.

Once the go-to drug of choice for eighties school kids, Tipp-Ex has come a long way since the scaremongering articles claiming it was the biggest killer next to the US crack epidemic.

Thankfully Tipp-Ex has left its hard-core days behind and has settled

Life Under a Sinn Féin Government

As a nation, we must brace ourselves for the possibility that fuck all will change.

back to its original use: a one-for-all corrective fluid capable of erasing all manner of scribbles on white paper. And now, thanks to a TikTok video one of our interns showed us on a joint break, we've got just the dental life hack for you.

By now you already know what we're going to suggest, but word count is word count so let's see how much longer we can hold your attention while we reveal exactly what you expect.

Paint your teeth with Tipp-Ex! That's it. That's our life hack.

Is Tipp-Ex still dangerous when taken orally? Fuck knows. I guess you'll find out. If you pop your clogs after using it then we can write a responsible article on the dangers of

Predictions for 2024

The US will invade somewhere cold and full of white people, just for a change.

Tipp-Exing your teeth, but for now, let's just roll with this for a while, see what falls out – it can't be any more dangerous than flying to Turkey to get them filed down to nothing and replaced with veneers in a medical facility with dubious online reviews.

NOTE: *WWN Life Hacks* cannot be held responsible for any damages caused by this article but would be open to hearing about it for future content.

MONEY

'SORRY, THIS TILL IS CARD ONLY' LOSER CASH CUSTOMER TOLD

A COMPLETE loser looking to pay for their goods with grubby old cash has rightly been told to wait in line while customers from the twenty-first century go ahead of him to use the card-only self-service till, *WWN* has learned.

Standing with his shopping and wallet in his hands like an absolute pleb, Cormac Murray observed the ease with which card-paying customers passed through the system, devoid of any human contact apart from the self-service till supervisor who shouts at the queue.

'Card only … is anyone card only?' the point-of-contact bellowed to a majority card-only queue, now looking in disgust at Murray.

'I guess this is exactly how Rosa Parks felt when she was told to sit at the back of the bus,' the 34-year-old son of two thought to himself, resenting

his decision to bypass the human-operated section of the supermarket. 'How is there only one cash till and why does it also give the option of card when the others are card only? Surely there should be a cash-only till too – I feel a little cheated if I'm honest.'

Finally attending the Neanderthal till, Murray cursed as his crumpled up €20 note was repeatedly regurgitated back at him by the machine like he had tried to poison it. The Waterford man was left impatiently waiting for the supervisor, who was now chatting to a fellow member of staff about last Saturday's work night out.

'Enjoy it while you can, ladies, before you all lose your jobs,' Murray muttered to himself, before reluctantly pulling out his contactless debit card to pay, returning his pathetic cash heap to his wallet.

MAN RUNS DISHWASHER WITH TWO TABLETS IN IT, JUST TO FEEL SOMETHING

LOST for something to do, Waterford man Eoghan Devlin has committed the afternoon to dishwashing like he's never dishwashed before: 'Going for gold,' in his own words.

Devlin, 37, has no real hobbies or interests outside of work, where he has been passed over time and time again for promotions, but is optimistic that using two Finish tabs on a single wash and splashing out on the 90-degree intensive cycle will fill the void in his heart, at least for an afternoon.

Having already run the dishwasher empty to ensure it's nice and clean, Devlin then added rinse aid into the rinse-aid thing and poured 'a shitload of salt' into the reservoir at the bottom, even going so far as to take out the filter

for the first time in ages and empty a load of old peas into the bin.

'You know how ladies like to have a big relaxing bath, cucumbers on the eyes, all that? Well, this is my version,' stated Devlin, shutting the door on his dishwasher, along with his hopes and dreams.

'I've even pre-soaked the plates and pots and pans, so there's zero chance anything comes out with crud still on it. No crushing disappointment here today, no sir. Just sparkling dishes and a renewed sense of purpose in life.'

Mr Devlin also stated that even if the glasses in the wash come out with water marks on them, it will give him the perfect opportunity to do a follow-up eco wash.

FAMILY

STUPID PARENTS WANT YOU TO COME OVER TO STUPID HOUSE FOR STUPID DINNER BECAUSE THEY LOVE YOU

LOCAL MAN Eamon Kilty's patience is well and truly worn thinner than a supermarket own-brand loo roll as he is forced, yet again, to field a request from his parents to partake in a family meal at home.

'Absolute ball-ache,' confirmed Kilty as he faced the prospect of being loved to such an extent by his parents that they frequently desire to see him in person, accompanied by a free meal.

'Hounding me so they are, it's like this 24/7. I can't do anything without them on to me. Like last month, I got a new job and they were all like "Congrats, let us take you out to celebrate". They sent me champagne and flowers and shit, they're just the worst,' explained Kilty, who can't catch a break from this parental pestering.

Kilty, who last accepted such an invite three months ago and only because he was too hungover to be arsed cooking for himself, continued to be hounded by his parents, with his mother placing needy demands on him via a WhatsApp message.

'Would love to have you over Thursday evening if free, curry night ❤' read the message, posing a huge inconvenience to Kilty, who planned on flicking through Netflix

> **'Hounding me so they are, it's like this 24/7. I can't do anything without them on to me'**

for hours before deciding not to watch anything that evening.

'They do it to my sister too, it's not normal at all. "Come over any time, we love you" – they sound so deranged, I'm embarrassed for them carrying on like that. And then it's one big guilt trip, like I don't have anything better to do with my time,' offered Kilty as he spent the evening picking his nose and arranging his snots into one ball of mega snot to rule over all other snots.

RELATIONSHIPS

LOCAL man Mark Reegan has reportedly not been seen out since he shacked up with that young one he met on Tinder, sparking fears as to whether he'll ever be out with the lads again, a WhatsApp group confirmed.

Mark, who would previously make it out for pints during hail, rain, sleet or snow, hasn't been seen since May following a successful date with some 'quare one' he met through the popular dating app.

'Cunt would turn up to the opening of an envelope,' friend David Mole

NO SIGN OF MARK OUT SINCE HE SHACKED UP WITH YOUR ONE

pointed out. 'You'd barely have uttered the "t" in pints and he'd already be shouting "What you having?" across the bar.'

Recalling previous relationship encounters, the group of friends realised this wasn't the first time

Reegan suddenly abandoned them for some bird he just met, referring to Jane, or Jenny, or whatever her name was, the last time Mark went missing for three whole weeks.

'It's bad form now,' insisted Gerry Hackett, who has known Mark since primary school. 'Fair enough he got himself a mot, but there's no need to just toss his mates aside like a hot snot, especially after the last one dumped him and he spent the next month ringing the lads in turn for pints every night – he can go fuck if he thinks he can just walk back into our lives when this latest one gives him the boot.'

Worryingly, Reegan was last spotted in Tesco buying original flavoured Pringles and a bottle of red wine, despite all his mates knowing he's a sour cream and onion with a bottle of beer guy himself.

'I WILL, YEAH!' STATES MAN WITH NO INTENTION OF DOING ANYTHING

EXPERTS have confirmed that whatever 'it' is, Dublin man Niall Burke isn't 'already on it', despite his claims to the contrary.

Burke has, in fact, spent the majority of the last 10 years claiming to be 'all over' a number of things ranging from work commitments, family chores and favours to his friends, neighbours and relatives, all the while being nowhere near all over it, under it, or anywhere near it.

In fact, a survey has shown that any time the 35-year-old actually completes a task to any degree of acceptability, it's been through a combination of delegation to others, last-minute scrambling or, indeed, just good old-fashioned sheer dumb luck.

'If he answers your request with "I will, yeah", then you'd better come up with a back-up plan,' explained a spokesperson for the International Dossers & Chancers Investigation Committee.

'The time you've allotted him to carry out whatever task or favour you need done will be spent playing Xbox or doomscrolling on his phone, combined with a healthy chunk of playing with his cat and a smidgen of sitting on the toilet for way longer

than doctors recommend. So maybe pick someone else to help you out, or give it an extra day or two to allow Mr Burke to get his finger out.'

We approached Burke for comment and he said he'd 'give us a shout later in the day'. That was two weeks ago.

Quotes of The Year
'Just a few more weeks until we can forget about this until next winter.'
– **Steven Donnelly** on the A&E crisis

RELATIONSHIPS

IS THIS PIECE OF HUNKY MAN MEAT REAL OR HAVE YOU FALLEN ASLEEP HEAD FIRST IN A SHARE BAG AGAIN?

WOW. It's like he's been waiting here for you your whole life. This beach feels like home ... like, you know it isn't home, but in this case your mind knows this is your home, weirdly. Which isn't good, because that sounds like dream logic.

And if you're implementing dream logic, José here isn't real, and he

won't be carrying you to your beach hut and four poster bed, folding you like orgasmic origami, sending you into such ecstasy you forget your own name.

You're face first in a share bag of Maltesers again, aren't you? Wearing the share bag like one of those oxygen masks that drop down on a plane in movies, which explains the wheezing – you thought it was the sound of the ocean's waves crashing behind José.

Look at him, so engaged and hanging on your every word. 'Speak to me again of all the true crime podcasts you listen to about murdered women that give you nightmares,' he says in

a smooth, deep voice that makes the hair on your arms stand on end.

Fight waking from slumber a little bit longer, maybe José still has time to tell you the names of the children you'll have together, and how he is financially independent because of his veterinary practice, where he rescues turtles from pirates who fire them out of cannons at rival pirates. OK, if you didn't know you were dreaming before, you do now.

Yes, you can definitely feel the drool amassing at the corner of your mouth as the remnants of Malteser crumbs melt onto your chin, but José doesn't care, he loves you for you.

HOROSCOPES

CULCHIE SURE DOES LOVE A GOOD TAROT READING

THE death of Mystic Meg has hit the astrology community hard, no more so than in rural Ireland where tarot card readings and fortune telling remain some of the most common pastimes among boggers of all ages.

No one quite knows when or why culchies latched on to fortune telling, but it remains the second-most popular belief system behind Catholicism, and the leading source of income in Ireland's nixer economy ahead of Reiki and 'cures'.

> **'You can ask them anything – am I going to die, when will I find love, will the guards ever find out about that thing I did?'**

'There's a whole lot of mumbo-jumbo and superstitious nonsense in this world, and the only way to avoid it is by going to an aul one up the road who will do the cards for you and give you a clear steer on things,' said one Waterford man we spoke to, who rarely makes a life decision without running it past a soothsayer.

'And you can ask them anything – am I going to die, when will I find love, will the guards ever find out about that thing I did, should I invest in crypto? They'll always have something to say on the subject, and

they're usually fairly spot on. Well, kind of spot on. Not spot on at all, in fact … usually way off the mark. But they'll have gotten some little detail vaguely correct, and that's enough for me.'

In some parts of the country, angel card readers outnumber teachers by ten to one. Even so, a culchie in need of help and advice can sometimes be forced to wait up to five weeks for an opportunity to have their palm read.

MAN CALLING ROADSIDE ASSISTANCE GLAD HIS FATHER DIDN'T LIVE TO SEE THIS

MAROONED on the side of the M9 motorway, somewhere around the Carlow exit, awaiting the arrival of a mechanic to take a look at his stricken automobile, Waterford man Eamon O'Carroll has tearfully expressed how he would be 'walking home in shame' by this stage if his father was still alive.

O'Carroll, 37, was on his way to Dublin to meet his new boyfriend for a day out in the city when the gearbox of his 12-reg Corsa suddenly became 'a box of neutrals', prompting him to limp to the side of the road and avail of the 24-hour roadside assistance provided by his insurance company, something that 'would have killed' his dad, if he wasn't already dead.

'Dad was grand with the whole gay thing, never phased him. But not being able to strip down and reassemble a gearbox on the side of the road, in the pissing rain? That he couldn't forgive,' O'Carroll told us as the roadside assistance lorry winched the irreparable car onto the tow bed.

'The man never brought a car to a garage in his life, and he certainly never asked anyone for help with fixing one. I remember we drove home from Cork to Waterford with a stop sign acting as a fourth wheel one day when we were kids. Another time, he miraculously turned water into diesel to bring us to Kilkenny after we ran out. So to see his son having to call for help for something as trivial as a collapsed gearbox would have gotten me written out of the will for sure.'

O'Carroll then refused a lift back to Waterford with the tow truck, instead staying behind to whittle a new car out of rocks and leaves, just like his father taught him.

GOLDFISH WOULD KILL ITSELF IF IT COULD

'YOU try being on your own for two years, swimming in circles around a bowl full of your own excrement and being fed once every few days without being able to top yourself. I yearn every waking second for the sweet release of death,' local goldfish Charlie stated today.

Ripped from an oxygenated pet shop tank full of friends and family members by Waterford dad Ger Hennessey, Charlie was gifted to human child and daughter of Hennessey in 2019, somehow surviving a series of diseases and near drops on the odd occasion when his tank water got changed.

'He dropped me into the sink one time while cleaning my tank and I thought I was free. My gills were gasping for water so much that I got aroused at the thought of dying,' Charlie recalls, now spitting out a lump of his own turd that he

mistook for a fish food pellet. 'I've tried bashing my head off the bowl, but the thing is so small that I can't get up enough speed to do any harm. I can't even hold my breath because I'm a fucking fish – just kill me already.'

Charlie is one of a long line of imprisoned goldfish who have been tortured by the Hennessey family, who seem to have some sort of sick infatuation with keeping an organism captive to satisfy their own delusional belief that their precious nine-year-old daughter can look after a pet.

'These people are monsters,' Charlie continued, before concluding, 'If they had any thread of decency in them, they'd flush me down the toilet – it would be a cleaner environment and I'd take my chances on making it to the sea.'

EXCLUSIVE

WOMAN'S BIOLOGICAL CLOCK REPLACED BY FOGHORN BLASTING 24/7

LOCAL woman Sheena D'Arcy is reassuring those around her that there is no need to panic, the loud and piercing foghorn sound is just her biological clock.

'Yeah, mad, isn't it? It just started up about a week after my last birthday,' confirmed the 39-year-old woman, shouting over the sound of the unrelenting din.

While women a decade younger than D'Arcy only have to contend with the unpleasant sound of a once-off daily

> **'To be honest, I don't even notice the foghorn anymore, but sure I don't need it, not with my mother there to remind me anyway'**

body clock alarm and stern warnings from doctors with the bedside manner of Harold Shipman that it's 'tick tock time', the Waterford native is now painfully aware of her geriatric status thanks to the 149-decibel strong blast.

'To be honest, I don't even notice the foghorn anymore, but sure I don't need it, not with my mother there to remind me anyway,' added D'Arcy, whose mother regularly places ads featuring her daughter's womb in the local paper.

Life Under a Sinn Féin Government

The name 'Saoirse' will top the list of most popular baby names for years, simply because you're not allowed put 'Up the Ra' on a birth cert.

Council Notices

Due to a double booking, the over-65s Choir of Hope rehearsal has been moved to Wednesday. The sold out How to Make Voodoo Dolls of Your Ex crochet class will go ahead as normal.

RELATIONSHIPS

MEET THE COUPLES WHO JUST SAID 'FUCK IT, YOU'LL DO'

THEY'RE the sort of people whose opinions are discounted when it comes to relationships, marginalised by those who hold on to the delusion that romance permeates every aspect of a couple's relationship and is sustained for life.

But now they've had enough of being silenced and ignored, and *WWN* is happy to do its part for a more inclusive Ireland when it comes to the full spectrum of relationships. Meet the couples who just said 'Fuck it, you'll do' and settled:

'We didn't meet at a "singles night". Technically, it was a "desperates night". It's similar but with a

desperates night, whoever you leave with you have to marry.'
– **Dave, 37, Carlow**

'He was very much my "back up" while I waited for my ex to see sense, but eight years later here we are. Imagine the effort of breaking up? Nah, we're in too deep now.'
– **Shona, 30, Galway**

'She's steady and reliable and she always goes down on me on my birthday. You can keep all that "love of my life" shite. Also, I can't afford to leave the house and move into an apartment by myself.'
– **Damien, 49, Cork**

'There was no going back after we met, not because I knew she was the one, but because I let myself go to complete shit. Sure like, who else would have me?'
– **Conor, 31, Wicklow**

'I leave the notion of romance for the movies. He has all his own teeth and he works in the civil service. That's all I need.'
– **Miriam, 41, Kilkenny**

'He does my head in, I actively hate him, he's a terrible father, but that's still not enough to make me go back on those fucking dating apps, not a chance.'
– **Paula, 34, Waterford**

'Romcoms have a lot to answer for. I spent years waiting for a "you complete me" speech, but himself has only said "I love you" once, and that was when he was drunk and he thought I was my sister.'
– **Fionnuala, 55, Louth**

'Ah, it's grand like, she's given up tearing into me when I fart in bed and if that's not love then I don't want it.'
– **Noel, 39, Kerry**

SOCIALISING

WHOLE VIBE IN CLUB THROWN OFF AFTER DECREPIT 30-SOMETHINGS ARRIVE

IT WAS unfolding like any other carefree and fun night in a city centre nightclub until it was gate-crashed by a group of 30-somethings in search of a post-pub closing pint.

Young and effervescent regulars had been lost among the throngs of sweaty dancers, but the killjoy capacity of quickly ageing 30-somethings 'utterly changed' the vibe in the club.

'They're hideous,' one 20-year-old said of the shambling crew of 30-somethings, dry-retching at the smell of Sambuca while showing less skin than an ISIS bride.

Straining at the volume of the music and shielding their eyes from a stray strobe light, the ungainly figures tried to 'blend in' by loudly discussing how young everyone was and how clubs were better craic in their day.

'They're in the weird limbo of not being old enough to be a welcome random novelty we can ironically join in a dance circle, it's just a bit … sad,' declared another bright young thing, slowly inching away from one of the 30s crew, who made a last order of 10 pints of Guinness with whiskey chasers as relentless drum and bass music punctured the air.

'THAT'S one of the good ones now,' local dad Tommy Kerns quickly pointed out to his daughter Maria as she unwrapped her brand-new air fryer.

Despite the €49.99 Tesco price tag still attached to the box, Mr Kerns explained that €50 is a good price for such a kitchen appliance, stating that there are far cheaper ones out there, but nothing is too good for his little girl.

'You'll never use a cooker again, swear to God,' Kerns went on, before spending several minutes listing off the vast array of food items one can cook. 'You'll save yourself a fortune on energy bills too. That €50 fryer will owe me … I mean, you, nothing after a few weeks, watch.'

Smiling politely at his latest gift, the 27-year-old thanked her father, wondering to herself where the 17-litre capacity monstrosity was going to fit in her already cramped apartment.

'If I move the €90 microwave and €60 blender Dad bought me for

DAD ALWAYS MENTIONING COST OF GIFT SO YOU KNOW HOW MUCH HE LOVES YOU

Christmas, I'm sure there'll be room,' she thought, remembering the value of each appliance thanks to his consistent habit. 'He only lets me know the cost because he wants me to know how much he loves me,' she reasoned.

'Right, we better go to the petrol station before I drop you back,' Kerns told his daughter, before resorting to his usual pre-lift-home jibe: 'You'll have me bloody broke at this rate, haha.'

RELATIONSHIPS

WOMAN WOULDN'T HAVE DATED MAN IF SHE KNEW HE USED E-SCOOTER

A LOCAL Dublin woman is once again asking for men to be more honest and upfront on dating apps after she discovered the man she was dating uses an e-scooter.

'I'd almost put it above needing to know if you're married with kids at this stage,' explained Sarah O'Halpin, who was crushed by the revelation that a man she had been dating for several weeks is one of 'those people'.

'Like, I tongued this freak to within an inch of his life on our first date.

> **'The broad shoulders, the fact he was 6' 3", that he cared for sick puppies in his spare time … it was all rendered meaningless'**

Nearly went home with him too – talk about dodging a bullet,' confirmed O'Halpin, dry retching at the thought of 26-year-old Kevin Downes scooting around town.

A survey of women in Ireland revealed e-scooter use ranks higher in a list of turn-offs than smoking, listening to Joe Rogan, still living at home with their parents, and being a conscript in the Russian Army.

Recalling the horror of seeing Downes arrive at their first sober, daytime date in a park on an e-scooter, O'Halpin becomes emotional.

 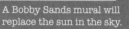
'The broad shoulders, the fact he was 6' 3", that he cared for sick puppies in his spare time … it was all rendered meaningless. I can't erase that image of him looking like an absolute eejit on his scooter,' O'Halpin said, a tissue crumpled in her hands as she wept.

Responding to the controversy, dating apps including Tinder, Bumble and Hinge have committed to banning accounts that don't formally disclose they're an e-scooter-owning dweeb.

SOCIAL MEDIA

SINGLE WOMAN JUST LOOKING FOR SOMEONE EQUALLY GOOD LOOKING TO APPEAR IN INSTAGRAM PICTURES WITH HER

'I DON'T care what they did in the past, how much money they have or whatever the issue is with them, I'm just looking for someone as good looking as me to appear beside me in Instagram photos,' single Waterford woman Denise Hurley tells *WWN*.

'Convict, homeless, has only one leg … it's no odds on me as all that stuff can be hidden using the right camera angles –

just as long as they have a perfectly symmetrical face, toned body, even tan and full head of hair,' continued the 28-year-old, who has had it up to here with 'Irish mongrels'. 'How hard is it to find someone who looks perfect but is a total trainwreck. I mean, we don't have to be romantic per se, they just need to accompany me in cutesy couple pics having perfect little picnics on the beach – that kind of shit.'

Exhausted from years of trying to find the perfect man, Hurley stated she doesn't even require the desired individual to speak English.

'He can be mute and deaf, fucking blind even – but not that obviously closed-eyed blind, if you get me. Just something good to look at and to match my own aesthetics,' she pleaded. 'I think women these days are too picky when it comes to men's personalities and I actually find it a bit shallow when a woman demands that a partner should make X amount of money and be faithful – I couldn't give a toss as long as he looks like a fucking ride.'

If you or someone you know fit Ms Hurley's criteria, please queue at the payphone box on Main Street, Tramore, this Sunday at 4 p.m.

BREAKING

FUCKING LEGEND STACKS SIDE PLATES ON DINNER PLATES

A COMPLETE fucking legend has reportedly stacked a variety of side plates directly on top of dinner plates, forcing everyone in the house to strain themselves even further when reaching in to grab a single dinner plate from the press, *WWN* has learned.

The stack of smaller plates, which weigh a tonne when you try to lift them with one hand, especially when bent down or reaching skywards, were kept in this unhelpful arrangement by housemates despite the annoyance, in

what is believed to be some form of deliberate karma.

'Well, I'm not fucking moving them to the side just so someone else

can come along and simply grab a dinner plate without having to go through the agony I've had to,' stated Deirdre Reilly, an otherwise normally functioning adult.

'I pulled a muscle in my neck one day trying to slide a dinner plate from underneath without knocking the side plates off the top,' said Martin Davids, another housemate.

In one passive-aggressive Post-it note last year, former housemate Geraldine Lyons attempted to solve the matter by scribbling a message, 'Please don't stack the side plates on the dinner plates,' which is believed now to be the entire reason why no one wants to resolve the issue.

'We kicked that stuck-up bitch out a day later,' a joint statement from the housemates said. 'No one tells us what to do.'

PEOPLE searching for healthy alternatives to snacks and drinks have been advised to seek out anything that comes in a very small portion, but that also costs more than anything else in the shop.

'For example, we've got this cold-pressed ginger and lemon juice right here. Each bottle costs €9 and holds less than would fill an eggcup,' said the proprietor of Healthy Hole, Waterford's premier health food outlet.

FANCY NEW JUICE COMES IN TINY BOTTLE SO IT MUST BE GOOD

'You can buy a two-litre bottle of Coke for, like, three quid, so by the law of opposites, this stuff must be pure rocket fuel for your health. Plus, only rich people can afford it, and

when was the last time you saw a sick-looking millionaire?'

This logic also applies to snacks such as protein bars and balls, which Healthy Hole offers for extortionate prices that almost guarantee their health benefits.

'Two matcha and goji berry balls for a tenner, you can't go wrong,' we were told.

'Think that's robbery? Fuck off and die in a hedge, you poor sick piece of crap. Do you even know what matcha is? Do you know what "cold-pressed" means? Go have a bag of chips and rot.'

Healthy Hole also offers a wide range of organic vegetables and promises that their produce isn't just dirtier carrots for twice the price.

Quotes of The Year 66

Unintelligible horseshit
- **Eamon Ryan**

CRIME

COUPLE CAUGHT SMUGGLING SNACKS WITH STREET VALUE OF €16 INTO CINEMA

GARDAÍ IN Dublin are celebrating an impressive seizure as part of Operation Snack Sneak, which has seen the force working side by side with cinema chains to bring an end to the scourge of people trying to avoid exorbitant snack prices in cinemas by smuggling in their own supplies.

Paraded in front of cameras in handcuffs like they were the Peru Two, Leah Feeley and Jack Nolan were arrested in the middle of a screening of *John Wick: Chapter 4* when one keen-eyed cinema worker noticed the presence of tubes of Pringles, Coca-Cola bottles and own-brand supermarket sweets with a total street value of €16.

'This is the largest seizure we've made to date and the individuals involved are looking at serious punishments,' explained arresting officer Garda Sean Shanahan.

'This operation wasn't easy and I thank the 47 colleagues who were part of this raid, and I apologise to the officer who had to perform the cavity searches, but the fact these sick criminals were storing as many as eight Freddo bars up there proves it was worth it.'

In future, Feeley and Nolan will be required to wear ankle monitors that beep upon entering a cinema, alerting staff to their presence. Staff will then place the pair through an X-ray

machine designed to identify smuggled-in snacks. Those wearing ankle monitors are then forced to strip down and wear clear plastic bags instead, making snack-sneaking impossible.

As if the dramatic arrest wasn't enough, another elite garda unit entered the cinema premises as part of Operation How Much? and arrested the cinema proprietor for charging €8 for some fucking popcorn.

80% OF VAGINAL DRYNESS CAUSED BY SOUND OF TWIN CAM REVVING, YOUNG MEN INFORMED

SCIENTISTS have discovered a direct link between the sudden plummet of a woman's sex drive and the appearance of a souped-up 2006 Honda Civic in a rural Irish town, *WWN* can report.

The study also shows that even the mere sound of a modified car exhaust is enough to put the majority of women off riding for days at a time, and that the noise of a dump valve can turn women off sex quicker than you can Google 'what's a dump valve?'.

Despite the overwhelming evidence that pumping thousands of euro into customising a Toyota Starlet is a surefire way to guarantee a life of celibacy, many motoring enthusiasts persist on cruising up and down town 'looking for skirt', while employing other techniques to hopefully woo a lady.

'The main reason people lower their seats so much when driving one of these things is to show as little of their faces as possible,' said one expert on automotive sexuality.

'And tinted windows help here too. So, on the off chance that a young lady can look past the clownish appearance and dreadful noise of your car, they won't immediately be

Dictionary Additions of 2024

'**Housing**': mythical structures worshipped by Irish people in much the same way ancient Egyptians worshipped cats.

repelled by the fact that it's being driven by a clueless teenager, or, indeed, a really clueless 30-year-old.'

If all else fails, boy racers are banking on the sexually aggressive humour of their bumper stickers to win over the hearts of young ladies.

ww news

Waterford Whispers News

SPORT

RUNNING

MARATHON RUNNER DISQUALIFIED AFTER TYING TWO CHEETAHS TO HER LEGS

A MARATHON runner who completed the 26-mile course in just one hour was stripped of her title this week, having been disqualified for strapping two African cheetahs to their legs, *WWN* has learned.

Teresa Ryan from Cappoquin in Waterford smashed the world record, making headlines across the world before adjudicators' attention were drawn to the rather large cheetah-print running shoes she was wearing, which were, in fact, actual cheetahs.

'Totally makes sense now that it's been pointed out to us,' an official

'She cut the two fuckers loose shortly before she reached the finishing line so no one would notice'

statement from the organisers of the local marathon read. 'Sure she was gone like the clappers of Jaysis down the street. We couldn't even see her she was travelling so fast.'

Ryan was later quizzed over the cheating accusations when gardaí were called to a backyard in Portlaw after a woman's chicken hatch was ravaged by what appeared to be two wild cats.

'She immediately owned up to cheating with cheetahs,' investigating officer Tadhg Moore told *WWN*. 'She cut the two fuckers loose shortly before she reached the finishing line so no one would notice

– smart enough now, when you think about it.'

Despite Ryan being stripped of the first-place title, she still received a trophy for chancing her arm, with organisers stating that 'it was a nice try all the same'.

RUGBY

JOHNNY SEXTON PUT OUT TO STUD

FOLLOWING the end of his rugby career, Johnny Sexton has been put out to stud, where he will sire the next generation of Irish 10s.

'With a state-of-the-art sperm extraction hose attached to his "how's your father" 24/7, we expect the Johnny production line to produce enough new fly-halves that every referee in the future will need therapy from the earaches they're going to suffer at the hands of junior Johnnies,' explained the owner of the stud farm, Middle Eastern billionaire sheikh Sean Sheedy.

It is believed Leinster have beaten out rivals and secured the first batch of what is being referred to as 'Johnny Juice'. While the price paid has not been disclosed, it is believed to be in the high six figures.

'Pure, unfiltered, expert game management – it's like gold dust,' a teary Leinster recruiter said as they hugged the vial of sperm tightly to their chest.

Rugby rights activists have been reassured that the conditions Sexton is being kept in are roomy and human-rights compliant.

'He has all the rugby kicking tees he needs, his diet consists of whatever they have at the Mace deli counter. Before bed we play YouTube compilations of him bollocking people out of it … he couldn't be happier,' added a stable hand.

Quotes of The Year

'Same again, landlord.'
– Brian Cowen

MAN HAS NO RECOLLECTION OF PUTTING CRICKET ON TV

'DID I blackout completely? Should I go see a doctor?' Waterford man John Waldron is struggling to explain how he's found himself watching hours of a test cricket match on his 50-inch TV, built to show the most adrenaline-pumping entertainment on the planet, which does not include cricket.

Keen to stress that he'd be the last person to watch 'English sports' that aren't soccer, tennis or rugby, Waldron has called on the manufacturer of his remote to fix the glitch that has affected his TV.

'There's just no way I'd switch this on myself. Maybe I was flicking and then I stopped on a funny ad, went to make tea and came back,' a bewildered Waldron said.

The explanation could lie in the fact that Waldron recently turned 40, an age at which sports such as cricket, snooker and lawn bowls start

to call to you like an alluring siren on the rocks.

'Nonsense, I'm not turning into my dad. If I was I'd be watching those Michael Portillo train programmes –

have you seen them? They're fantastic! Honestly, well worth a wa… Oh God, no!' Waldron added, before looking down at his feet to find he's wearing socks with sandals.

GAA

BLIND PRICK OF A REF CLEARLY TAKING BRIBES COMPLAINS OF ABUSE GAA REFEREES GET

A GAA referee whose family is up to their necks in all sorts of shady and shameful stuff, if you believe local gossips, has meekly claimed that he has stepped away from refereeing due to the abuse he receives as well as a lack of support from the GAA.

'This corrupt little shite would want to take a look in the mirror, he's only retiring because we all know he was taking bribes. You only need look

at the semi-final there last year and that last-minute 45,' said one local, referencing a game his club narrowly lost by 27 points.

'Abuse? What abuse is that inbred cunt getting? Show me one example. Slimy, no-good liar, ruining our game with his antics,' confirmed one man, who added that he knows where referee Gerry Maskin lives.

Maskin, a referee of 20 years, is believed to be part of a growing cohort of officials undermining the ethos of the GAA by making plainly unfair and biased decisions in games, which leave supporters no choice but to jump on the bonnet of his car as he attempts to leave after games.

'Officiating in this country is a joke. If they played the game to a high level at all themselves, they'd know taking stray elbows as you try to referee a game is part and parcel of GAA. We don't want this turning into soccer, we've got to protect the game,' added another GAA stalwart.

NURSES, doctors, teachers, engineers and full-time mad bastards have downed tools across Australia today and, in the process, have wiped several billion off the value of the Australian economy.

With the backbone of many Australian industries composed almost entirely of relations Irish people had to wave off as they emigrated from home, it is expected that for the duration of Ireland's FIFA World Cup 2023 game against Australia, the host

AUSTRALIAN ECONOMY BROUGHT TO STANDSTILL AS IRISH IMMIGRANTS WATCH AUSTRALIA GAME

country risks the imminent collapse of key infrastructure and services.

'There won't be a dairy cow or vegetable picked on Australian

farms for 90 minutes, or three days when adjusted for the possibility of an Irish win,' explained a leading Irishologist.

The 83,500 capacity venue for the match, Stadium Australia in Sydney, had been criticised by Irish fans as an insultingly small stadium, with only 150,000 able to get their hands on tickets. The number of Irish people claiming to have attended the match will increase tenfold in the event of a victory.

'He's bleeding out, God damn it! Help me, Chip-van … or whatever weird impossible to pronounce Irish name you have,' one nurse cried out to her colleague Siobhan Hayes, who was glued to a nearby TV.

As is Irish custom, no pressure has been applied to Vera Pauw's stars but, at the same time, Ireland fully expects to win the tournament.

WOMEN'S SPORTS

'I CAN'T WATCH THIS SHITE' SAYS MAN WATCHING WORLD CUP FULL OF WOMEN REFUSING TO DIVE

Life Under a Sinn Féin Government

SF

Consistency will be achieved by Sinn Féin using 'the previous government' excuse for everything too.

UNABLE to take the ridiculous display that is the FIFA Women's World Cup seriously, local man David Limpken is on the verge of throwing his TV out of the window, so incensed is he by the fact some people have the brass neck to call what he's watching 'football'.

'Not one of these professional athletes is acting like John Wick removed their eyes with a rusty spoon when they receive the faintest of touches from an opponent,' an incredulous Limpken said, as he watched the much-fancied USA team take on the Netherlands.

Throwing his hands up in disbelief and disdain, Limpken couldn't fathom how the players seemed completely ignorant of the finer techniques involved in synchronised three-metre springboard diving, which is so very common in the men's version of the game.

> **'If I wanted to watch a game that isn't stopped every two minutes for phantom dismemberment of limbs, I'd watch chess'**

'If I wanted to watch a game that isn't stopped every two minutes for phantom dismemberment of limbs, I'd watch chess. Where's the prima donnas? Where's the blatant cheating? Where's the eejits rolling around like a bunch of girls? And by girls I mean highly paid male professional footballers,' a fed-up Limpken said.

Elsewhere, another soccer fan said he felt 'unwelcome' in stadiums after he tried to get several homophobic and racist chants up and running in the crowd to no avail.

Bill's Political Tips

When you're confronted by a homeless father of two, simply say, 'Counterpoint: have you seen how healthy the latest GDP figures are?' without blinking.

WOMEN'S SPORTS

WOMEN'S SPORTS JUST YEARS AWAY FROM BEING REFERRED TO AS 'SPORTS'

RESEARCHERS at MIT tentatively announced that 'womanny' sports could achieve the title of 'genuine sports' in a matter of decades, if not years.

'We live in an age where we can grow artificial organs and food, where AI is advancing civilisation, so there's no reason not to believe that lady golf could be referred to as "golf",' an excited lead researcher at the university told *WWN Sports*.

'Girly sports are currently in the 'ah, bless them' sphere of sports, like men's over 40s five-a-side football. But with a little extra effort by everyone, we could all pretend they're deserving of equal respect,' added the researcher.

Milestones to be cleared for such a status to be achieved include your uncle no longer saying, 'Jaysis, she's pure brilliant, and not just for a girl,' and your boyfriend actually watching the camogie or the WSL.

'The women's Six Nations? No, it's shite,' said one female respondent to a survey connected to the MIT study, single-handedly forcing researchers to revise their predictions to the mid-2130s.

CONOR McGREGOR LEAVES FANS CONCERNED AS HE HASN'T BEEN UP IN COURT FOR AN ENTIRE MONTH

FANS OF former UFC champion Conor McGregor have voiced their concerns online after noticing he hasn't been up in court in almost an entire month.

Regularly staying in the news due to assaults, traffic offences and generally being a gobshite, McGregor's well-paid PR team have somehow managed to fill the dead air with a flurry of tabloid fluff pieces lifted from his social media profiles, showcasing him as a doting father and not someone who causes mayhem between losing fights.

'Usually there are rumours of him impregnating fans or assaulting old men or women, but nothing like that has surfaced in almost four weeks,' one die-hard fan told *WWN*, who would literally die for McGregor if he asked him to. 'Bring back the old Conor any day, with his boisterous goings-on and his gas shenanigans.'

'I fear he might level out now and become one of those boring martial artists who just does it for the sport and not the fame and fortune,' another fan said. 'Another week of no court appearances and I'm out.'

'He could have fallen in with the wrong crowd of wealthy business people, who can simply just hush things up with money,' added one commentator. 'I preferred him when he was hanging around with his mates linked to cartel figures, whose rivals were petrol-bombing his pubs, now it's all yachts this, hanging out with celebrities that. For the love of God, Conor, just smash up a hotel room or something!'

GAA

INQUIRY LAUNCHED AS GAA GAME PASSES WITHOUT ASSAULT OF REFEREE

GARDAÍ are liaising with the Waterford county board and the GAA after it emerged that a referee carried out his duties on the field without suffering serious assault.

'This isn't normal, it's not acceptable. We will look into it and punish the adult men who refrained from punching and kicking a referee,' said a spokesperson for the GAA's Just Letting Off Steam unit.

An incident is said to have failed to occur as the referee called a number of fouls, gave a penalty, and issued three yellows and a black card during a Junior B match.

'When I hear stories like this, I feel like we're losing what makes this sport and the wider GAA community great. These young lads playing now, not one of them even threatened the referee verbally. No one told the ref they know where he

> **'You need to root out this problem before it gets any worse'**

lives. It would make you cry,' said one spectator at the match.

'You need to root out this problem before it gets any worse. You can't call yourself a good club man if you don't call out players when you see them accepting an on-field decision like a well-adjusted human with no underlying anger management issues,' added another

spectator, who called on the GAA to issue lifetime bans to those not involved in despicable incidents of assault.

UPDATE: The referee in question is said to be recovering at home but fears he may never referee again if he's not subjected to violence. 'Usually I'd be in A&E of an evening. I've no idea what to do with all this free time and feeling in my face,' said the referee.

Quotes of The Year 66

'Oh, now I see why Ryan quit.'
- **Patrick Kielty**

Things We've Learned as a Nation

Natural gas is a valuable resource! We probably could have done something with that knowledge.

HORSE RACING

LUCKY WATERFORD MAN WINS €5 MILLION ACCUMULATOR BET AFTER CORRECTLY PICKING HORSES KILLED AT AINTREE

ECSTATIC Waterford man Daniel O'Faylon has left bookies reeling this week after successfully choosing the correct horses to perish at this year's Aintree festival, *WWN* reports.

The accumulator bet on racehorses Hill Sixteen, Dark Raven and Envoye Special won Mr O'Faylon €5 million, a first in sports betting, which usually requires punters to bet on the winning horse and not the ones that die for the sport.

'Since 46 horses died on UK tracks so far this year, I said I'd try and predict which ones will be euthanised at Aintree,' the delighted 53-year-old explained. 'Yeah, some people may say it's a cruel thing to do, but not as cruel as stud farms here and in the UK sending tens of thousands of racehorses to meat factories every year because they simply can't run fast enough.'

Meanwhile, police arrested 118 protesters at the racing festival after they delayed the prestigious Grand National by breaching security fences and locking themselves to jumps, much to the disgust of the alcohol-fuelled crowd of wealthy middle-class spectators, millionaire trainers and billionaire racehorse owners who bayed manically from the stands.

'They should have been shot when they tried to scale that fence,' one Irish horse trainer told *WWN*, not talking about the horses for once, and still furious that the flagship race was delayed by several excruciating minutes which gave his investors mini heart attacks. 'Have these idiots no idea the amount of money riding on these horses?'

> ### 'Since 46 horses died on UK tracks so far this year, I said I'd try and predict which ones will be euthanised at Aintree'

Things We've Learned as a Nation

It's possible to go 120kph on a pothole-ridden rural backroad if you just believe in yourself enough.

FOOTBALL

INTER MILAN TO FACE 115 BREACHES OF FINANCIAL FAIR PLAY IN CHAMPIONS LEAGUE FINAL

AFTER their convincing win over city rivals AC Milan, Simone Inzaghi's Inter Milan now know the only thing that stands between them and Champions League glory is Premier League side 115 Breaches Of Financial Fair Play.

The plucky underdogs, otherwise known as 'The Breachers', triumphed against all odds over kings of Europe Real Madrid with a 4-0 second-leg win in their home stadium of The Inflated Sponsorship Paid By Company Owned By Same People That Own The Club Arena.

'I can't believe we're this close to a historic treble, and it's all a result of slow, methodical processes such as hiding top-up payments to former managers and our owner hiding the fact that he was pumping money into the club via payments to companies who would then sponsor the team with said money,' said one Breachers fan, approaching joyous delirium.

'Bald fraud, is it? Haha, I don't think so,' added a fan of a club that is accused of endless actual fraud.

In what is sure to be one of the most-watched sports events of the year, Breachers could go into the game having already bought the Premier League and FA Cup, paving the way for a potential treble – a prospect even neutrals are excited by.

'Call me a romantic, but I'd like to see the club that spent £1.5 billion on transfers in the last decade win the Champions League. It's a feelgood story,' said one neutral.

Bill's Political Tips

No matter how obvious it shows that you are lying, always deny everything until the very last moment. And, if caught, just say you have no recollection.

MAN HAS NEVER PLAYED SPORT BUT BOY HAS HE OPINIONS ON IT

FOR someone who displays an in-depth knowledge of the history of sport, as well as what appears to be a keen eye for managerial tactics, you'd think that Waterford man Mark Smyth would voice his opinions where they matter most.

'Yeah, I save my wisdom for when I'm in the pub with the lads, or when I'm on the sideline watching one of my kids playing. There's some lazy little fuckers who just don't have the motivation, and boy do I let them know about it,' said Smyth, owner of an athlete's mind but not an athlete's body.

'Can you believe there are some eight-year-olds who don't know the meaning of "adopt a harder back line and sweep out the wings with short-ball play"?' Fucking chancers, letting us all down. I tell the lads down the boozer, between chats about how the standard of play in the lower half of the Bundesliga is a joke, and about how women's GAA is alright to watch if there's absolutely nothing else on telly.'

Amazingly, Smyth's knowledge of sport has been acquired without ever so much as kicking a ball in his life, something that he puts down to years of being angry about everything related to the subject.

'I know everything except how to be happy when someone wins. It's not in my DNA,' he admitted, while trying to suppress his delight at a good

performance by his favourite team, just so he can point out their flaws in an exhausting hour-long rant.

BREAKING

PUTIN FINALLY ADMITS IT WAS WRONG TO POSE FOR PHOTO WITH CONOR McGREGOR

ON THE anniversary of his military invasion of Ukraine, Vladimir Putin is finally ready to apologise, but not for the reprehensible crimes related to his 'special military operation'.

'I should have known better. I should have done research into who he was before agreeing to a photo,' a regretful Putin said today as his critics once more brought up

the photo that continues to haunt him more than the brutal massacre of Ukrainian innocents: his 2018 World Cup final photo with Conor McGregor.

'I'm not one who finds it easy to apologise or admit a mistake or a war crime, but on this occasion I couldn't in all good conscience continue to act like this photo was something to be proud of,' admitted Putin.

'If I had known of his behaviour, the accusations against him, and how shit his whiskey is, would I have posed with him? No, 100% no. Did you see that Steve Jobs whiskey ad thing he did? Cringe. More cringy than the speeches where I paint myself as the victim,' conceded Putin, in a rare moment of genuine contrition.

While many people have been waiting years for him to admit fault for a number of things, including his crackdown on LGBT rights, the jailing of political rivals, and countless killings, some say the McGregor apology is enough.

'It seems like a small gesture, but it means a lot to me,' said one Irish person who has been maintaining that McGregor is a 'dose' ever since he first set eyes on him.

Life Under a Sinn Féin Government

SF

Hospitals will be overrun with voters suffering from shock after the director of a party, who is responsible for illegally converting a flat he rents out, does not solve the housing crisis.

WOMAN GRABS HIKING STICKS, SETS OUT ON PERILOUS TREK ALONG PERFECTLY FLAT FOOTPATH

DONNING expensive outdoor gear like she was about to leave a Himalayan basecamp, local woman Tina Murphy grabbed her pair of trusty hiking sticks to brave what is to be her biggest challenge to date: the perfectly flat ring road encircling her local town.

Making sure to let everyone know about her upcoming excursion, the perfectly able-bodied Murphy messaged anyone who would listen,

stating she should be back in an hour or two, depending on the conditions.

Now walking along the concrete path, her professional mountaineering sticks clicking with every stride, the 45-year-old squinted at the glaring sun with the air of a 1940s expedition up

K2, minus the sherpas to lead the way.

'Seriously, where the fuck is your one going with the bloody hiking sticks?' one passing motorist asked, wondering if he drove through a portal somewhere along the way.

Stopping for a second to catch her breath, the daughter-of-two looked back at the route she just travelled, all 500 metres of it.

'Glad I brought these now; I probably would never have made it across that speed bump pedestrian crossing safely without them,' she said to herself, proud of the progress she made as cars whizzed by on the Tramore ring road, motorists rubbernecking at her ridiculousness.

Finally making it up the 0.005% incline to 'the top of the road', Murphy turned on her heels.

'They say going back down is the hardest part,' she told herself, before making the perilous journey back home.

GAA

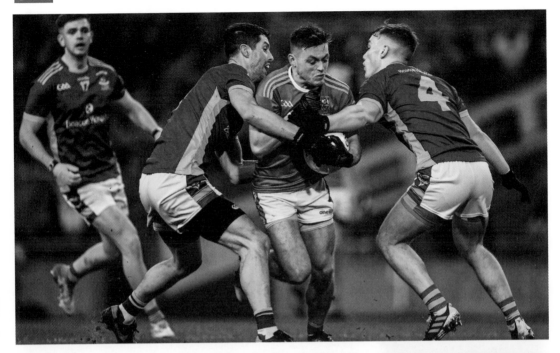

NEW FOOTAGE SHOWS KILMACUD CROKES HAD 148 PLAYERS ON PITCH DURING GLEN 45

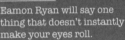

IT'S the GAA controversy that refuses to die. Appeals and counter appeals have been filed to counter objections to counter objections, newspaper columns comparing it to apartheid South Africa have been written, and 'Dubspiracy' is the number one trending topic across all social media platforms.

Those hoping the scandal would run out of steam and calls for the All-Ireland club final to be replayed would fade away will not want to see the new footage of that last-ditch Glen 45.

'Holy shit,' remarked the head of the GAA's Scandal Containment Unit as they laid eyes on a never-before-seen angle of the action, which clearly shows Kilmacud Crokes had not 16, not 17, but 148 players on the field.

'Look, umpires miss things, refs miss things … if we were to replay games over every little thing, we'd never get anything done,' suggested one GAA fan, who denied being one of the 75 Crokes players bussed onto the pitch unbeknownst to the referee.

> **'Look, umpires miss things, refs miss things … if we were to replay games over every little thing, we'd never get anything done'**

'No, I was one of the lads parachuted in.'

Glen club officials have asked for their appeal to bypass the GAA central council and go straight to the Hague, even though it doesn't have jurisdiction over the matter.

'You don't ask a post man to investigate a murder, so it's only fair the Hague investigates a crime against humanity,' said one Glen man. 'And I say this as a neutral with no dog in the fight and no bias, but those extra players should be shot.'

UPDATE: Kilmacud Crokes deny submitting an extra two appeals in their initial appeal against Glen's appeal.

FOOTBALL

VAR REPLAY CONFIRMS LINEKER ONSIDE

BBC football presenter Gary Lineker is no longer facing outside pressure to be sacked from his job after a VAR check found his tweets, which decried the Tory government's proposed anti-asylum seeker laws, were fully onside.

The proposed laws, brought forward by aspiring Disney cartoon villain Suella Cowardwoman, have already been rubbished by legal

experts for breaking international law and contravening the European Convention on Human Rights.

'If you look here where Gary says, "These people are human beings," he's clearly onside, a full yard or two behind the last defender of the Tories celebrating cruelty like it's a virtue, and not giving a shit that 187 child asylum seekers remain missing after being placed in the care of the Home Office,' confirmed the VAR official.

'Another angle here shows that if the Tories can call people fleeing war and persecution an "invasion", then Gary can say maybe that's not a great look.'

Lineker, who famously never received a yellow or red card

during his career as a professional footballer, dodged a booking despite not agreeing with PM Rishi Sunak's gleeful warning that if a vulnerable person is placed under slavery conditions and trafficked to Britain, they'll get no help.

'We know we say woke cancel culture is ruining the world, but we're going to dedicate our front page to trying to get Gary Lineker cancelled from his job of doing the football,' confirmed the *Daily Mail*, incensed at such a flagrant public display of empathy towards refugees.

'Everyone at the Beeb must remain politically neutral and unbiased,' added the *Mail* of the BBC, which is now run by the Tory donor Richard Sharp who helped Boris Johnson get an £800,000 loan in the weeks before Sharp was named BBC chairman.

FOOTBALL

ONLY A MATTER OF TIME BEFORE UNDER-9S REALISE LOCAL COACH HASN'T A CLUE

HUNGOVER and running out of cones, local father and under-9s football coach Ed Ganley is facing up to the realisation that his limitations as a coach could be exposed at any point.

'Go and run around with the balls there, boys,' Ganley told Mellick Green Rovers under-9s in between dry retching, in a scene we imagine is reminiscent of when Pep Guardiola trains with City.

With no coaching badges and the shameful secret that he was woeful at

football himself, Ganley reckons it will take just one rebel among the group to become bored with his methods for a mutiny to take place.

'I didn't even want to coach them. Jack's dad dropped out last minute after that car accident put him in hospital, which is selfish if you ask me. I don't know what to do other than make them run until they're too tired to disagree with me,' Ganley relayed as he surveyed the uncoordinated and unfocused training session in front of him.

Ganley had thought the initial purchase of a clipboard would suffice as a false visual indication of his vast experience and knowledge, protecting him from the reality that when it comes to football, he only repeats things he's heard on football podcasts.

'Coach Ed, we've done dribbling in and out of cones loads, can we learn about how to collectively activate the press and play possession-based football? Counter attacking is all well and good, but Jack hasn't the pace or hold-up ability,' asked one little prick whose parents shouldn't let him watch so many YouTube tactical breakdown videos.

DIE HARD fans of Katie Taylor and all she has achieved in sport were understandably emotional on Saturday night in the wake of her defeat by Chantelle Cameron.

Those painful scenes were nothing, however, compared to the eye-ache they developed when having to see Conor McGregor on their screens.

PAIN OF TAYLOR DEFEAT ECLIPSED BY PAIN OF SEEING McGREGOR RINGSIDE

'I was watching from behind the couch through my hands, not because I found Katie's loss distressing, it

just pains me to see that muppet McGregor's mug ringside. Surely there should have been some sort of gobshite warning?' explained one superfan, who has watched every professional bout in Taylor's storied career.

'Oh God, I can't watch this, it's too much,' wept another fan as the camera showed McGregor for the 253rd time during the 10-round lightweight fight.

'I've seen men die in the ring and that's more pleasant than the sight of that hopping mad cretin,' added another boxing fan, who successfully received a refund from DAZN citing 'visual terrorism'.

Capitalising on the stomach-turning effect McGregor has on many Irish people, pay-per-view providers have revealed that they will offer a special 'Dose Free Broadcast', which will blur out McGregor, for the reasonable price of €89.99 in the event of a rematch.

GAA

WATERFORD HURLERS STAND BY DECISION TO JOIN BREAKAWAY SAUDI GAA CHAMPIONSHIP

Saudi GAA Championship

THE controversial Saudi Arabian senior football and hurling championships are to go ahead as planned this winter despite protests of 'sportswashing', and will include several of Waterford's most middle-of-the-road players in the tournament.

'I think it's a wonderful opportunity to bring the uniting power of hurling to an oil-rich Middle Eastern kingdom,' said Martin Campbell, who will captain the Waterford Saudi hurling team in their kick-off match against Doha in November.

'It's certainly got nothing to do with the boatload of cash that arrived at

my house the other day. This is about wanting to play hurling in the off-season, in a desert, for the benefit of all the Saudi hurling fans who would go without otherwise. Honest.'

Campbell was pressed on his opinions about the Saudi government's human rights abuses, and whether he feels that he and his players were being used as part of a wider scheme to make Saudi Arabia seem like a fun, friendly place where no journalists get chopped up and no gay people get stoned to death.

'No, this is 100% on the level, just like the golf tour,' argued Campbell, who has been asked this

> **'I think it's a wonderful opportunity to bring the uniting power of hurling to an oil-rich Middle Eastern kingdom'**

same question twice and is already getting sick of it.

'If I wanted to play in an environment where women are second-class citizens, where gay people are discriminated against, and where lads get viciously attacked for no good reason, I'd have stayed in Waterford. I'm here so the fans of GAA have something to enjoy all year round,' he concluded.

The first game of the €400 million Saudi GAA Championships takes place on 11 November at 3 a.m.

Council Notices

Just a reminder that anyone with an illness is asked to avoid hospitals for the next month or six, just while they work through a 20-year backlog.

WW news

Waterford Whispers News

PROPERTY

EVICTIONS

'IT'S A CIVIL MATTER': GARDAÍ IGNORE LANDLORD BULLDOZING HOUSE WITH TENANTS IN SITU

AS THEIR screams slowly faded to muffles, drowned out by the crumbling concrete and roar of his JCB, landlord Patrick White blissfully ignored all regulations and law pertaining to evictions while gardaí watched on in case the tenants somehow managed to retaliate.

'Our hands are tied here as it's a civil matter,' local Garda Terry Holden told WWN as the landlord shovelled a mix of children's toys and rubble towards where the family room was once located.

The forced eviction, one of dozens happening at any one time across the country today, came after the tenants, who rumour has it were foreign nationals, failed to leave the property after White gave them a 30-day notice five minutes ago.

'That's notice to quit,' White bellowed over the diesel engine digger, making sure this reporter phrased the act appropriately, as stipulated by government advisors when addressing evictions in the media. 'They said they have nowhere to move to, but that's not my problem, so I had no other choice but to do it the good old-fashioned way. I'm sure there's plenty of room for them back in their own country!'

> **'They said they have nowhere to move to, but that's not my problem, so I had no other choice but to do it the good old-fashioned way'**

Ignoring the tenants' calls for help like it was a 999 call, gardaí watched on as the family slowly climbed out of what remained of the house, and recited the phrase 'it's a civil matter' again before pointing out the amount of paperwork involved in such an intervention.

'Best focus our time on other things, like someone smoking a joint, or a learner driver being unaccompanied. Besides, the landlord seems to be renovating the place now anyway, so they haven't a leg to stand on,' one garda pointed out before heading off to double park on a double-yellow line outside a chipper for some lunch.

Bill's Political Tips

Remove all pictures of you and your buddy in school, college and the accountancy firm from Facebook before appointing them to that State board.

RENTING

LANDLORD HAS BROTHER MOVING HOME FROM AMERICA ... AGAIN

WATERFORD landlord James Caughlan has regrettably informed the tenants at one of his properties that they need to vacate the premises, as he has a brother coming home from America who needs somewhere to stay, and while Caughlan would rather keep his source of income from the house, this is family, damn it!

'Believe me, I'd much rather keep you guys in the house and have the cash coming in every month, even if it is well below the market value and caps prevent me from hiking it up any further,' sobbed Caughlan as he served the family of four with their marching papers.

'But my brother, what's his name, he's on his way back from, eh, New York, and I promised him he could stay in the house free of charge. Silly me! Anyways, he's packing his bags to

move here as we speak, so maybe you should start packing yours too, eh?'

Although little is known of Caughlan, he appears to come from a large family, all boys, and seems to be the only one who didn't emigrate to

America for a few years only to return in need of accommodation.

In fact, *WWN* learned that one of Caughlan's brothers arrives back from the States almost every two years, and they always seek residence in one of his many rental properties around Waterford.

'What can I say, I'm all heart,' explained the landlord.

'If a brother is coming home, he gets a house. I'm like Oprah. Now excuse me, I have to get this family out and paint the house for my brother coming home. And put in bunk beds for his seven, eh, friends. Oh, and if you see my brother here in a few weeks and think that he's Brazilian, that's nonsense. He's just been in the States for a long time, and he's picked up quite the tan ... and forgotten how to speak English. It happens!'

DEVELOPER FINDS €100K BROWN ENVELOPE IN JACKET HE HASN'T WORN IN AGES

IT'S JUST one stroke of luck after another for a Waterford property developer this week, who found a big wad of cash in an old jacket just after hearing the news that he would also be getting a windfall of money from An Bord Pleanála (ABP) as part of a

€1 million fine levied against them.

Sean Harris, owner of the Harris Group, had a smile on his face after hearing that he will receive €9,875 in compensation from ABP because of a backlog in processing developments, which he will now just 'blow on

drink and drugs' after finding €100k in crisp €500 notes in a padded envelope while trying on a jacket he hasn't worn since he went to the Galway Races in 2019.

'I'll be honest with you, I don't remember who I was supposed to give this to or who gave it to me, or if I found it, stole it, got it as a bribe, any of it,' said a delighted Harris, who intends to needle ABP for more money now that they're on the ropes over the 'fast track' applications scandal.

'It's not like I need to bribe anyone anymore because the things we used to bribe for are all pretty much legal these days. In fact, as you've seen this week, we can now sue for damages if planning isn't processed fast enough!'

Meanwhile, the hits keep on coming for the owner of Harris Group after an American fund agreed to buy up an entire housing development outside Waterford off the plans, without so much as a brick laid, prompting the nation to state that it warms their hearts when nice things happen to nice people.

EXCLUSIVE

WHERE ARE THEY NOW: GHOST ESTATES

THE lack of available housing in Ireland today is a far cry from the surplus stock found scattered around the nation in the years following the financial crash. These so-called 'ghost estates' comprised approximately 30,000 empty or unfinished units that lay eerily empty in boarded-up developments from Cork to Donegal.

Fast forward to today, and these forlorn and pitiful entities no longer feature in our countryside, so where did they all go?

'When the economy collapsed, it was like the bit in *Ghostbusters* where they shut off the containment unit. Ghost estates immediately started popping up everywhere,' said Fr Eamon Gherkin, senior ghost estate advisor to the Vatican.

> **'When the economy collapsed, it was like the bit in *Ghostbusters* where they shut off the containment unit'**

'As with most things that happen in this world, the Church immediately saw an opportunity to make some money out of it. So we set up the Official Holy Estate Exorcism Squad, a crack team of priests that included myself, only a young priest of 65 at the time. We said we would remove any ghosts or evil spirits from these estates for a small but substantial fee, and return them to economic prosperity as and when the market turned.'

Along with his fellow exorcists, Fr Gherkin toured the country performing complex rituals aimed at bringing the scourge of ghost estates to an end. They were finally successful in guaranteeing a significant return to foreign investors, who bought the properties at fire-sale prices from NAMA before sitting on them for a decade until the demand for homes had reached the point that they could charge whatever they wanted for them.

'And, of course, we made out like bandits, too. Now, did we actually *do* anything in the process, or would these vulture funds have made just as much money by gouging the Irish people in the long run anyways?' mused Fr Gherkin from aboard his yacht *The Ave Large One, Maria*. 'Who's to say? All I know is that we got ours, Ireland is free from ghost estates, and if anyone is finding it hard to buy a home, light a few candles next time you're at mass. Can't help but notice that the lighting-candles revenue has dipped lately, maybe another recession would help you people remember who's really in charge around here.'

Although they're now long gone from Ireland, many say you can still hear an eerie wail as you walk past housing developments that were once considered 'ghost estates', although closer inspection usually reveals this to be homeowners who are realising that their 'newly finished' houses were built to 2006 standards and then given a coat of paint, and are almost entirely riddled with pyrite.

RENTING

BEAUTIFUL PHOTO CAPTURES RETURNING FLOCK OF LANDLORDS TO RENTAL MARKET

WHEN AMATEUR photographer Dylan McCartlin went out for his morning walk, armed with his SLR camera, he never imagined in his wildest dreams that he would capture one of the most elusive sights in Irish wildlife, according to the government at least: the Lesser Spotted Vilified Landlord.

'I didn't realise what they were at first, until I heard one of them on the phone to Newstalk saying they were an accidental landlord,' McCartlin said of the sighting, which happened close to 7 a.m.

'Some mornings I don't get any decent photos – it's just depressing tents along the canal – but apparently these guys are endangered so it was really thrilling to snap them,' McCartlin added.

The incredible formation of landlords would not have been possible were it not for government intervention in helping them reclaim key nesting spots – properties people live in – by introducing an end to the eviction ban. The freeing up of these nesting spots will encourage a fresh migration of landlords to watering holes such as Daft.ie.

'I'm just a bit annoyed at myself because I didn't capture the Minister for Housing in the image,' said McCartlin of Darragh O'Brien, who was laying a breadcrumb trail of €800 million worth of tax breaks in a bid to lead landlords back to their historic grazing grounds: high-rent-yield properties, which would only make homes for prospective home owners if they fell into the wrong hands.

Landlord-spotting nerds have argued that McCartlin's photos are nothing special, as such flocks have been easy to spot on Airbnb or happily perched on a vacant property.

PERSON *of the* YEAR

WWN

BILL
BADBODY

LANDLORD | BROADCASTER | PHILANTHROPIST | POLITICIAN | BUSINESSMAN

EXCLUSIVE

'I FIND IT DISGUSTING 99% OF THE POPULATION OWNS 73% OF THE WEALTH' – BILL BADBODY

Following a new Oxfam report which found that 1% of Irish society now owns more than a quarter of the country's wealth, *WWN* property editor and multi-millionaire landlord Bill Badbody explains why he is disgusted that the elite don't own more.

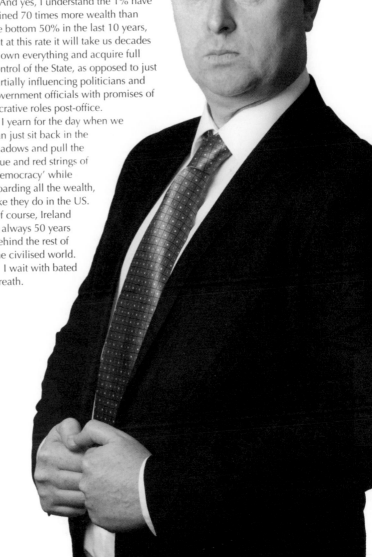

FOR the love of Bono, where do I even start with this nauseating fact? How can so many poor people own such a large proportion of the country's money and continue to get away with it? Most of these people can't even afford to live, yet somehow they have accumulated nearly three quarters of the nation's wealth. This is dangerous and also very unfair on us elite – the minority.

For too long, wealthism has been festering in Irish society. Investment funds and corporate landlords like me have been vilified in the media. Somehow now *we're* the bad guys, while the 99% continue to get free council homes, healthcare, discounts on their energy bills and, even more infuriating, rent vouchers. Thankfully on the latter most of my properties are cash only and not registered with the RTB, but still, it's the thought that hurts.

Despite their faults, the housing minister, along with local councils, are doing a fantastic job of keeping housing supply down and allowing us to keep rents high – I'll give them that – but it doesn't cover up the fact that

the plebs still own the vast majority of homes in Ireland, and that's criminal.

And yes, I understand the 1% have gained 70 times more wealth than the bottom 50% in the last 10 years, but at this rate it will take us decades to own everything and acquire full control of the State, as opposed to just partially influencing politicians and government officials with promises of lucrative roles post-office.

I yearn for the day when we can just sit back in the shadows and pull the blue and red strings of 'democracy' while hoarding all the wealth, like they do in the US. Of course, Ireland is always 50 years behind the rest of the civilised world.

I wait with bated breath.

Things We've Learned as a Nation

There's no limit to how much Cadbury can shrink their bars, we'll just sit there and take it.

Quotes of The Year

'It's the "sharing" part of power-sharing that confuses us.' **– DUP**

HOUSE BUILDING

GOVERNMENT TO BUILD ONE GIANT HOUSE WITH €476 MILLION UNSPENT HOUSING BUDGET

MINISTER for Housing Darragh O'Brien unveiled plans for one gigantic house to be built out of this year's unspent housing budget, which stands at €467 million, *WWN* reports.

An imposing two kilometres high and four kilometres wide, the aptly named 'social house' is expected to do exactly what it says on the tin and help house tens of thousands of families currently on the waiting list for social housing.

'Delighted to announce this new project. Of course, we could have used the money to do up the 4,500 council houses that are currently vacant or, indeed, actually build homes from the €476 million housing budget, but just look at how cool this house is – it's huge!' O'Brien was in awe at his plans, which will see the house built on a 'commuter belt in Donegal'.

'Imagine the 800,000 plus young people currently living at home with mammy and daddy moving in here, it'll be great! We've even built a lovely big shed out the back to put the 100,000 Ukrainian refugees we'll have by this time next year.'

Beaming with pride, the housing minister gloated his department will still actually meet their 24,600 annual target despite the underspend, pointing out the unspent money was set aside for social housing, freeloaders waiting on housing lists, those kinds of people.

'Targets are targets,' O'Brien pointed out, patting himself on the back. 'Shame about the low earners waiting on homes though, we'll get around to them at some stage in the next 20 years. You know, when the population is six million and mass homelessness is the norm like it is currently in the US and the UK.'

With almost a million people looking for homes in Ireland and just 24,600 being built every year, O'Brien hasn't ruled out a *Battle Royale* type scenario in the near future, where people fight to the death for homes.

> **'We've even built a lovely big shed out the back to put the 100k Ukrainian refugees we'll have by this time next year'**

STUDENT ACCOMODATION

STUDENT WONDERING IF LIVING IN TENT MIGHT BE IMPACTING COLLEGE WORK

AWARE that such excuse-making could gain him a reputation as a work-shy layabout and all round Negative Nellie, local tent-dwelling student Fionn Dalton remains unable to shake the feeling that perhaps his focus on college would be greatly enhanced had he a room in a house or apartment to call his own.

'I'm at every lecture, doing my assignments, but I suppose I sort of question sometimes if brushing my teeth and spitting into a drain every morning amid dropping temperatures is the best way to start your day,' explained the Cork native, now residing in a bush in Dublin near his university.

Careful not to cause anyone offence, Dalton was keen to stress he was not slagging off tent-dwelling, but he would very much be open to not being a homeless student if anyone could help him out.

'Plugs, that's the main thing to be honest,' added Dalton, growing tired of his laptop's battery dying as he carried out college work at the desk portion of his tent.

However, not everyone is buying Dalton's sob story.

> **'Back in my day we didn't have laptops. We just arranged small stones on the ground to look like a keyboard and we were happy'**

'You think that's bad? Back in my day we didn't have laptops. We just arranged small stones on the ground to look like a keyboard and we were happy. No moaning from us,' offered one Celtic Tiger-era student, who lived in a nightmare time of banks running huge ad campaigns encouraging students to openly lie as they applied for loans, which were handed out like condoms at Freshers' Week.

In a statement, both the Department of Education and Department of Housing have confirmed they are aware of the problems some students still have in securing accommodation, but what do you expect them to do about it?

FINANCE

'TOO RICH FOR MY BLOOD': MONOPOLY MAN DRIVEN OUT OF IRISH PROPERTY MARKET

'IT'S WORSE it's getting,' confirmed real estate investor Rich Uncle Pennybags, signalling bad news for the health of the Irish property market.

Quotes of The Year

'This glamping is shit, isn't it?'
– Brian Boru

Dictionary Additions of 2024

'Consequences': unpleasant punishment as a result of illegal or amoral actions taken. Example: politician resigning, charged by authorities after wrongdoing. Currently not in use in Hiberno-English.

'I used to own some property in Rathgar, Kildare Street, Ailesbury Road, you name it, but the market's gone so deranged that I've been priced out of the brown places too,' said Pennybags, who walked away from an auction after bidding for a two-bed in Kimmage reached €500,000.

'I was the original vulture fund, but it's too rich for my blood. Look, I loved nothing more than tearing down houses and building hotels, but this is a young, foreign-pension fund manager's game these days,' said

> **'I loved nothing more than tearing down houses and building hotels, but this is a young, foreign-pension fund manager's game these days'**

Pennybags from the driver's seat of his 1940s Kurtis Kraft Midget Racer.

Pennybags has advised first-time buyers that what they're buying might be dark-blue property prices today, but that is certain to change.

'There was a real pleasure in driving into Dublin availing of free parking and eyeing up what to buy next, but the prices have hit a peak … there's a crash coming and there's no get-out-of-your-mortgage-debt-free card.'

WOODIES UNVEILS LINE OF HOME TOOLS WHICH CAN ALSO BE USED BY LANDLORDS TO THREATEN TENANTS WITH

SPOTTING a potential new customer base previously uninterested in DIY tools, Woodies have launched a range of tools specifically for landlords to wield when threatening and trying to chuck out tenants during illegal evictions.

'Historically we've aimed our products at gardeners, handy men and those looking to hang up a picture, but based on viral videos of deranged landlords waving tools at tenants, we knew it was time to expand our horizons,' explained new-business manager Rory Boggins.

Displayed at the front of all outlets, the 'Landlord Range' includes a circular saw, hammer, and all manner of tools that would aid any landlords looking to intimidate tenants they view as subhuman.

'We've made the saw blunt, but it's three times as loud, so if you're a landlord who is seeking to traumatise a mother and her three kids, we've got you covered,' added Boggins.

Meanwhile, B&Q is reporting record sales after cashing in on the lucrative 'burying a body up the Wicklow mountains' gangland market.

NEW GOVERNMENT SCHEME WILL ALLOW FIRST-TIME BUYERS TO BRIEFLY STARE AT HOUSE FOR SMALL FEE

A NEW scheme aimed at getting first-time buyers on the property ladder, albeit ten floors below the first rung, has been proudly announced by the Department of Housing.

In lieu of a functioning housing market, the Department has proposed new measures which could be launched in a glitzy fashion and provide government TDs with opportunities to get photos of themselves in hard hats.

'It's exciting. A recent survey showed that two in five young people thought a house was a work of fiction, like a unicorn, Bigfoot or Niall Collins' humility. Seeing the expressions on the faces of the first people to avail of the "Look for a Buck" scheme was a joy,' said the Department's Head of Vague Targets We Never Seem to Meet.

Stares at homes will be limited to one person per couple, and will last for a maximum of 30 seconds, after which time the person can draw the house for their partner from memory, but they may not keep the drawing.

'It had these walkie things that made you taller,' said one hopeful homeowner, describing seeing a set of stairs for the first time.

'Unlike the previous 419 amendments we've made to the Housing for All plan, which we said was the only solution to the housing crisis, this might *actually* make a difference,' concluded Minister for Housing Darragh O'Brien.

EXCLUSIVE

'WHAT'S THE POINT IN BEING A LANDLORD IF I CAN'T EVICT PEOPLE?'

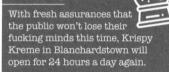
Furious at a new law banning the eviction of tenants until the end of March, *WWN* property editor and head of the Irish Landlord League Bill Badbody asks, 'What's the point in being a landlord anymore if I can't evict people?'

IT'S ALL I get up for in the morning: the frosty air, the camaraderie with the bailiffs, the screams of children as we rip their parents from their tiny bedrooms while we litter the front yard with smelly toys, dated flat screens and grubby buggies. How I'll miss the distinctive sound of the

locks being changed, the chuckles from snack-box munching gardaí as they flank our raid and enforce our investment fund's legal documents. That's all gone now. Christmas won't be the same this year.

Don't get me wrong. This government has done plenty by

keeping supply down and allowing rents to skyrocket without too much interference. The local councils too, by not bothering to use up their budgets to build social housing and their blatant boycott of collecting vacant property taxes. I appreciate that. But this? This draconian ban has my long line of landowning ancestors turning in their Protestant tombs.

What is a landlord without an eviction, only a landpleb? We're in this for the money, yes. But more importantly, we're in this for the power. If I can't just evict someone paying below the highest rent I see on Daft.ie and replace them with higher-paying tenants, then I don't know if I even want to be a landlord anymore. If landlords aren't allowed to evict tenants, then where are people looking to rent homes expected to find one? The government? Please. Eviction is the natural order of life: one pleb goes and the other comes and pays a higher rent. Implementing eviction bans only stops the natural pleb flow.

Sure, I'm salivating at the thoughts of all the bars and restaurant units that will come to market now that they're at risk of folding thanks to inflation and energy bills. And I'm sure my councillor friends won't have any issue granting me planning permission to change those premises into build-to-rents that I'll rent back to them for silly money for 10 years before selling them off for

> **We're in this for the money, yes. But more importantly, we're in this for the power'**

Life Under a Sinn Féin Government SF

Investing in flood defences to protect against the deluge of tears bursting forth from the offices of the *Irish Independent* is essential.

a fortune – that's going to be very exciting, yes. But my main love is kicking the poor out into the rural Irish wilderness where they belong so that wealthier tenants can replace them and drive up property prices and rent yields.

This isn't just a ban on evictions, this is a ban on good old-fashioned fun.

ON THIS DAY

𝔚aterford 𝔚hispers 𝔑ews

VOL 3, 20156136 | SATURDAY 28 JANUARY 1989 | 90p

Local Dunce Fails To Make The 'A Class' Following Entrance Exam

A COMPLETE and utter gombeen is to join an entire class of like-minded fools after failing to make the A class in his new, soon-to-be secondary school, *WWN* has learned.

Taking his entrance exam early on Saturday morning, Cathal Moore struggled to correctly answer the questions in a one-for-all exam designed to segregate the dunces from the smart kids, in an age-old tradition carried out by CBS Tramore.

'I was out in the pub with my parents all evening drinking buckets of Club Orange, and I had nothing to eat only King crisps and pink Snacks,' Moore said, attempting to excuse his poor performance by blaming his hard-working parents, who like to let off some steam every weekend. 'We didn't get home 'til three in the morning and they brought half the pub back with them, so I got very little sleep 'cause one of their pub mates woke me up by pissing on my bed.'

Destined now to leave school at 16 for a trade, Moore will be kept in the dreaded B class – a class of children which the school system will no doubt stereotype as a shower of dopes for the remainder of their secondary school lives.

'Alienating the B pupils as a lower form of intelligence from the get-go will set them up for their future place in society,' Brother Damien told *WWN*, wondering which of these little rogues he'll be beating with a belt come September. 'We also lump the poorer kids into B too, even if they do well in the exam, as you couldn't be giving them notions,' he added, while simultaneously promoting the children good at hurling to the A class.

Meanwhile, it was decided that Johnny Dwyer, Moore's fellow sixth-class student and best mate, will be kept back a year, after his failure to cover any of his copy books in brown paper.

Continued on Page 2

RENTING

LANDLORD JUST LAUGHS WHEN TENANT ASKS FOR RTB REFERENCE NUMBER NEEDED TO CLAIM €500 RENT REBATE

A LOCAL Landlord's January blues all but disappeared after a hilarious interaction with one tenant who was asking for information which would help them apply for a €500 tax rebate.

'Ah stop, you're one funny fecker. Has anyone told you you'd make a great stand up?' landlord Peter Price told tenant Michal Nowak when he enquired about the RTB registration number, which is a required field to complete when claiming the rent rebate from Revenue.

'Registered? RTB? Hahaha, are you taking the piss? Why do you think

> **'Registered? RTB? Hahaha, are you taking the piss? Why do you think you've been paying cash all this time?'**

you've been paying cash all this time?' informed Price, just one of thousands of landlords making it impossible for tenants to claim a rebate they are entitled to.

Repeatedly telling his tenant he is a 'gas man', and not just because the suspected gas leak in the flat remains unfixed, Price reminded Nowak that his living situation is due to Price's impressive generosity.

'Don't rock the boat, I could be charging you a lot more than I am. Well, not legally speaking, but … Sure I'm losing money on this place, there's no money in the landlord game,'

explained Price, who has nothing to show for his landlording only a steady stream of rental income and multiple assets worth in excess of €2 million.

Meanwhile, Nowak proved his comedic sensibilities by confirming how amusing it would be for the RTB and taxman to learn of Price's existence, which prompted the landlord to tell a funny joke about 'the tenant fucked out onto the street by a private security firm'.

Things We've Learned as a Nation

There's no talking to Dubs about coddle. If they want to eat boiled sausages, just leave them to it.

Council Notices

Just a reminder that bagged dog poop goes in the bin – not on top of the bin, on the ground beside the bin, or hanging on a twig near the bin. It's confusing, we know.

ww news

Waterford Whispers News

WWN GUIDES

RETAIL

ARGOS CATALOGUE: OUR FONDEST MEMORIES

'SO LONG and thanks for all the fishing equipment and cheap engagement rings' – this was the message from the Irish public to catalogue superstore Argos in response to the announcement that the company was folding its reasonably-priced tents in 2023.

One cannot mention Argos without mentioning the Argos catalogue, and although the printed version was cancelled during the pandemic, memories of the thick, treasure-laden tome live long in our hearts.

The stuff

So much stuff! The eighties generation, growing up in what were the worst economic conditions Ireland had ever faced, had never seen so many things in one place. We could not even conceive of owning the items in the Argos catalogue. In fact, Ireland didn't have a branch of Argos until the mid-nineties, so we couldn't have bought any of it, even if we had the money to. But the sheer amount of stuff created a consumeristic hole in our hearts that decades of buying shit has yet to fill.

The porn

Ireland in the eighties had no pornography, so an Argos catalogue wasn't just a list of things that looked like the prizes on *Bullseye*, it was as close to a *Playboy* as many of us could get. The models posing with the home tanning beds, the bare leg reaching out from behind the foldable bath screen, the lady bending over to use the Phillips standing hoover – in an Ireland crushed by the oppressive

fist of the Catholic Church, the Argos catalogue was like a depraved weekend in Amsterdam.

The hope

The Argos catalogue signified hope for us all. Hope that one day we'd live in a home with enough material possessions to numb the fact that our parents were only still together because divorce

> **'So long and thanks for all the fishing equipment and cheap engagement rings'**

wasn't legal yet. Hope that someday we'd have a job that paid us enough money so we could immediately exchange it for something we didn't need. Hope that maybe, just maybe, our parents would notice that we'd left the catalogue open with Boulder Hill from *M.A.S.K.* circled and they'd take the hint. When you don't have stuff, all you have is hope. And as we enter an Ireland without Argos for the first time in nearly 30 years, we must hold on to that hope. And head up to Newry once in a while.

ENTERTAINING

HOW TO HELP GUESTS GET THE HINT IT'S TIME TO FUCK OFF HOME

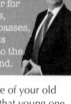
ENTERTAINING friends in your home can be a lovely and rewarding experience, but for the 98% of Irish people who think you're mad if you enjoy that sort of stuff, it's important to remain fluent in 'fuck off home with ya'.

The subtle art of heavily hinting that it is now time for your guests to make like the French Revolution and head off should not be underestimated. But how does one hint that you just want to be left alone in peace to take a satisfying

dump in your toilet while scrolling on your phone?

The following phrases are bullet-proof hints that won't fail to make your guests feel so uncomfortable and unwelcome that they'll only stay another hour or two before finally leaving:

- Suppose you'll want to beat the traffic?
- Where does the time go?
- You've fucking eaten me out of Cadbury Mini Rolls. They were a 12-pack for Christ's sake. What, do you think I'm made of money? G'way and fuck off with ya.
- What's that noise? That'll be the nuclear war siren. You'd best be off home to say goodbye to your loved ones. You can't hear it? Oh God, it's doing my head in, the noise of it.

- What was the name of your old school bully? And that young one that did the dirt with your ex? And your old boss handsy Andy? Well, it's just I forgot I was having them all over now in the next five minutes so you'd probably want to rush off, be horrible for you to run into them.
- Leave? Now? Ah Jesus no, stay. We were just about to stick on *Mrs Brown's Boys*. Yeah, we have all the DVDs. Ah no, where are you going?
- Have you seen my ingrown toenail? Now honestly, you think you've seen an ingrown toenail, but this fella? Oof, more pus than a cat shelter. C'mere now, you have to get down on the ground to really get in close.

SEX

SO YOU'VE FOUND YOUR GIRLFRIEND'S VIBRATOR, HERE'S WHAT TO DO NEXT

YOU'VE just found your girlfriend's vibrator. After fainting and falling unconscious next to her bedside locker, once you regain your composure you will start to wonder what this means for you and what's next.

- Check the UN charter on human rights. Has she violated yours by seeking pleasure elsewhere? You're fairly confident you know the answer but just double check: Google 'could a vibrator be my children's real father?'

- Double check the Ts&Cs in your relationship. Yes, you're allowed pull the lad off yourself, but where is it written that she can get a buzz from the buzz-buzz?
- Shun all urges to talk to her about it or suggest incorporating it into your sex life together.
- Treat a woman's infrequent desire to seek pleasure with herself as the selfish rejection of you that it almost certainly is.
- Next time you have sex with each other, make a constant, low-level buzzing noise while

weeping and saying, 'Is this what you want?'
- Write to all major battery manufacturers pleading with them to cease production immediately.

CULTURE

THE CIRCUS IS IN TOWN: HERE'S HOW YOUR KIDS NEED NEVER KNOW ABOUT IT

AS A parent, it's your responsibility to ensure your children live an existence that is as culturally enriching as possible, and that they experience as many new things as they can as they make their way through life.

It is also, on occasion, your responsibility to deny them all of these things so that you can have an afternoon to yourself. It's not too much to ask. You work hard. You shouldn't have to be down €100 and a whole Saturday because there's a damn circus in town. Avoid it by doing the following:

Limit the number of posters your kids see

Even in this day of targeted online advertising, most circuses still rely on plastering the town with posters and flyers. While parents struggle to keep their kids from seeing things online, it's really easy to make sure they don't see stuff in the real world.

Just don't take them to places where posters are. Can your kids drive? Are they allowed walk through town on their own? Didn't think so. Keep this up for a fortnight and they'll never know the damn thing was in town to begin with.

Tell them the truth about the circus

Maybe the kids see a poster. Maybe some little rat at school blows your cover. Now it's time to sit your kids down and tell them the truth: the circus claims hundreds of lives every year, mostly youngsters.

Lions escape and eat kids, motorcycle stunt acrobats careen out of control and plough into crowds, clowns just straight up kidnap children. Maybe throw in a bunch of animal abuse accusations while you're at it. Sure, circuses have cleaned their act up in recent years, but there's bound to be an elephant that gets the odd kick here and there.

Does your kid still want to go to a show like that? What kind of monster are you, Timmy!?

Up the screen time

Kids don't want to go to the circus. Kids want tablets and videogames and telly and snacks. Parents try to keep this from them to make sure they develop and grow. But how about, for just one day, you let your kids go nuts? Watch YouTube from morning to night? Show us a kid that would trade that for a circus.

Now you're free to spend your Saturday doing whatever you please, in a place that has no clowns. And you didn't have to admit that you didn't want to go to the circus because you're scared of clowns. Because of the thing. The thing that happened. The thing with the clown. The thing you don't talk about. Relax, it's all good … until the next circus arrives. They can't get you until then.

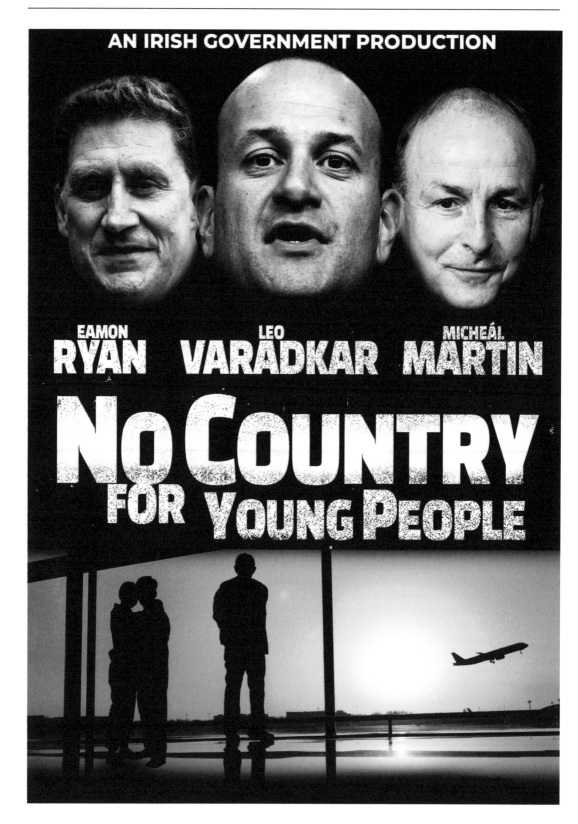

DRINKING

THE IRISH AND TEA: A COMPLETE HISTORY

IT'S HARD to imagine that there was ever a time you could pay a visit to an Irish house and not be offered a cup of tea, but that was very much the case as recently as the sixteenth century, when importers began to ship the product from the Far East for the first time. Although initially they were only bringing it to aristocrats in Britain, how it got to your mam's house is another story entirely.

1650: Tea is initially introduced into British society as a medicinal drink, believed to ease aches and pains and afflictions. In colonised Ireland, the Irish people do their best to ensure their English invaders have plenty of aches, pains and afflictions that need easing.

1680: Tea begins to make its way out of English kettles and into Irish homesteads, following looting raids on the Crown's forces. Initially, the Irish didn't know what to do with the strange leaf, but nevertheless found great sport in using the drink to lampoon their oppressors. 'Look at me, I'm an English prick drinking his tea, sip sup sip!' they would laugh, while secretly growing fond of the beverage.

1760: Almost a hundred years later, the Irish are well on their way to becoming the tea-loving nation we are today. This, however, was a cause

of strife as the British could easily identify rebels by checking their homes for tea that had clearly been stolen from English camps. 'Hey, that's mine. My cousin Seamie in China sent it over to me,' the Irish would plead, while being led to the gallows.

1800s: Throughout the 1800s, tea became an integral part of the Irish rebellion against the hated British. Every meeting, every plot, every raid, every funeral had to include a nice cup of tea for everyone involved. Burn a settlement? That calls for tea. Get routed by the English? Tea. Have a genocidal famine inflicted on you, forcing you to flee your homeland? Ah sure, you'll have a cup of tea before you go.

1921: With a new century comes a new independence, with Ireland finally free from the yoke of British rule. Ireland, on the cusp of a treaty that would see it rule their own lands,

reaches a stalemate over the issue of British tea still being available in the soon-to-be Free State. De Valera was OK with it; Collins wanted a complete break from it, cold turkey, let the English take their tea and shove it. You may have thought the Irish Civil War was over the north of Ireland, but this is the real story.

1945: Although the Tea Civil War has cooled off, a new batch of fighting breaks out over whether the nation should adopt loose tea as standard, or switch to these new teabag things. Purists are adamant that loose is the way to go. Separatist baggers say otherwise. Blood must be shed.

1980: As the Troubles in the north continue to wreak havoc on life in Ireland, tea remains the only consistent in this crazy world. Protestants, Catholics, Free Staters and Nordies alike enjoy a nice cup of tea, while they complain bitterly about how much they all hate each other's stinking guts.

2007: Post-Good Friday Agreement and bang in the middle of the Celtic Tiger, Ireland begins to get some notions about itself. Coffee creeps into the market, edging tea out of the equation. The idea that Ireland may be about to drop tea as its beverage of choice sends seismic ripples through world markets. Many believe this was the moment the global economic crash began.

2019: On an all-new high, the Irish demand for tea forces Chinese farmers to expand their lands to ensure supplies are adequate. 'Bulldoze a few of them wetlands, sure the bats that live there will find a new home,' they are told. 'Watch out there, some of them seem to have runny noses. Plough on, you're grand.'

Present day: Tea remains a cornerstone of Irish existence, to the point where any house that doesn't at least offer a visitor a 'drop in their hand' can be hit with fines of up to €500 and a month in prison.

DRINKING

'Give me a shout when you're back on it'

Reassuring your friend that you'll be the first one to celebrate with them when they get over their addiction and finally get back to good old-fashioned scoops.

'All drink? Or can you have a few pints?'

Always good to make sure they're not just off spirits and wine, as they turn into absolute wreck-the-heads on both.

'I heard the first 30 years off drink are the toughest'

Offering up some in-depth knowledge you may or may not have heard somewhere is a great way to keep up their optimism.

'I completely respect your decision and support you fully, but if you so much as ask me to socialise with you somewhere other than a pub, I will treat it as the biggest inconvenience anyone has ever had to endure'

Fairly self-explanatory this one.

'GIVE ME A SHOUT WHEN YOU'RE BACK ON IT': THINGS TO SAY TO RECOVERING ALCOHOLICS

GIVING up an addictive substance can be one of the most difficult things an addict can go through, which is why we at *WWN* have compiled a list of things you can say to recovering alcoholics to show you understand what they're going through.

'Yeah, but my stag is coming up so you needn't think you're putting a dampener on that – the fucking state of ya, like!'

Bill's Political Tips

Just one fixed pothole in five years could be the key to re-election.

Lines will need to be drawn early and your friend will respect you for your honesty – it's refreshing, unlike zero alcohol drinks.

'Jesus Christ, you were hardly any craic on it. Now what are you going to be like?'

Sometimes you just have to say it like it is.

HOME FINANCES

HOME FINANCES

A 'HEAT YOUR HOME THIS WINTER GUIDE' FROM OUR POVERTY EXPERT, VISCOUNTESS VERA DU BOIS III

IT'S the little things, like small adjustments and a look at switching providers, which can make the world of difference to your bank balance as we enter a winter in which increased energy prices and consumption could spell disaster for already struggling individuals.

Following the lead of other publications, we have enlisted the help of an expert on energy usage and heating who knows what ordinary people are going through. Introducing our new cost of living correspondent, Viscountess Vera Du Bois III.

Bills? Oh, I don't do any of that, that's for the staff to worry about.

I know how tough people are finding it. The drop in temperature has meant we've had to move my jewellery collection into a temperature-controlled room – nothing worse than putting on one of your blood-diamond necklaces and getting a little shock from how cold it is against your skin.

Reduce wasteful heat usage practices: I find moving from your summer house in November to your small, unassuming woodland cottage with 12 guest chalets certainly helps.

Blankets: It's not all about throwing another log on one of your 27 fires.

Life Under a Sinn Féin Government

SF

History teachers will save hours upon hours when Irish history books are replaced with the words, 'The feckin' Brits are at it again.'

Use your private jet to fetch blankets from your Austrian ski lodge. But if, like me, you make a mistake and forget you actually left those blankets in your New York penthouse, simply get the gamekeeper on your winter estate to kill a few of your llama and use the wool from their carcasses.

Draughts: Get one of your servants to lie across the bottom of a door to form a human draught excluder.

SMILING AT OLD PEOPLE SO THEY DON'T THINK YOU'RE ABOUT TO ROB THEM

PUNY OLD people walking along the street always look scared and vulnerable, glancing up with their pathetic faces, attempting to drag a sympathetic look out of you in the hopes you don't batter them to death and take their wallets, which is why *WWN* has put together this handy guide on smiling at old people.

Practice, practice, practice

First, remember that not all smiles are reassuring. Some smiles can reveal your true nature and terrify old people. Over-smiling in a maniacal fashion is a no-no, so practising your fake smile in the mirror is a good idea. It's all in the eyes: don't look too intently, relax your brows, unclench your fists, stop snarling and frothing at the mouth. Anything longer than three seconds is too long; a glance will be enough to put them at ease, along with one of a selection of greetings.

Greetings

'Grand day' or 'miserable day' will suffice in all scenarios. Expanding your greetings beyond this isn't advised, but if you are caught short for something non-weather related to say, then using the good old-fashioned 'hello' is acceptable. Make sure to pronounce 'hello' fully. Never say, 'How ya getting on?' or 'Well, how's it going?' as these terms can be confused with 'Gimme your fucking money or I'll beat you to a pulp' – best keep it simple to avoid unnecessary confusion.

Wave

A solitary wave can also be used while passing. Most old people are hard of hearing and need an additional visual element to cement the greeting.

> **'Gimme your fucking money or I'll beat you to a pulp'**

A slight wave with one hand will come across as passive and safe. The floppier the hand, the better. Taking the effort to wave shows how soft and caring you are. With the right smile, greeting and wave combo, your passing pensioner will be set.

PLEASE NOTE: This guide will also work for those of you wishing to rob old people.

Dictionary Additions of 2024

'Novid': the state of mind of someone who forgot the last three years happened so they stand right behind you in a queue coughing their balls off.

DINING OUT

'IT WAS LOVELY, THANKS': IRISH GUIDE TO MAKING A FOOD COMPLAINT

Bill's Political Tips

Don't denounce virulent and open racism before double checking that supporting it isn't a big vote-getter.

THANKS to its sparse population and just two degrees of separation between residents, the island of Ireland has always been a country afraid of carrying notions, with its people prepared to do anything but complain about poor service, poor commodities or, indeed, poorly run government departments.

The hospitality sector here is no different, and sometimes Irish people need a little advice on how to stand up for themselves and complain, so here are some guidelines for making a food complaint in Ireland.

'It was lovely, thanks'

Said with zero commitment and without looking the server in the eye, letting the waiting staff know

you weren't entirely happy with your meal can easily be decoded in this one simple phrase. This, and the fact you haven't even touched the meal itself, may prompt them to ask if you're sure everything was OK, to which you must reply, ''Twas grand.'

Take to social media

Without even waiting for the server to take your plate, log on to your social media app of choice and set your privacy settings to 'public' before writing a lengthy review about the food you just had and the 'lack of service'. Stop the server and ask if you can take a picture of the meal they're removing and upload that with your 2,000-word post. Tag the business

and post the complaint for the entire world to see.

Ignore all confrontation or questions from the business

Depending on how busy the restaurant is, they may take some time to respond to the complaint, which you could have just sorted out there and then, but instead it has garnered huge interactions online, doing untold damage to the reputation of the business. It's important here to ignore all pleas of reconciliation from the restaurant and offers of vouchers or compensation. Let your social media post do all the work and, *voilà*, you've successfully made an Irish-style food complaint.

SOCIALISING

YOU'VE MET A FELLOW IRISH PERSON ABROAD BUT IT TURNS OUT THEY'RE A DOSE: YOUR NEXT STEPS

YOU THOUGHT a polite 'Ah yeah, that's gas, imagine – two Irish people on holiday in one of the world's most frequented tourist hotspots, what are the chances?' would be the end of it, but no, this Irish person you've met while on holiday is intent on draining the life force from you.

It's one thing to meet a dose, but it's another to trick them into thinking it

was their idea to end the conversation and fuck off. Here's how to shake an Irish dose you've met on holiday:

- Slowly drop your accent over several sentences until you seamlessly transition it into an English brogue.
- Are they taking a genuine interest in you and asking you lots of questions? Turn the tables by doing the same, only go harder – Irish people can't help but become suspicious at someone's interest in their life.
- Say you're Bertie Ahern's cousin.
- Tell them you work for Revenue or Social Welfare or, better still, a new super-department called Revenue Welfare.

- If they're with their partner, start pretending you recognise them from that stag party in Vegas, you know the one, Steo's stag party. Sure it was fuckin' wild and you're glad they sorted out all that business with the strippers and the cops.
- Introduce an intense love of Conor McGregor into conversation. Note: this could result in them fleeing instantly or attempting to fuse themselves to your skin in an effort to form a symbiotic organism.
- Start complaining about immigration from Albino.
- Ask about Saipan and just take the opposite side to them.

SEX

NOT SURE IF SHE FAKED AN ORGASM? HALT EVERYTHING AND HIT HER WITH THESE QUESTIONS

SHE'S made all the right noises, moved in all the right ways, and certainly seems to have climaxed, but how can you be certain your partner has actually enjoyed herself in bed? You can't, can you? She might just be faking it to spare your feelings. Time to find out. But how?

Bring it up in casual conversation immediately

There's no time to wait around to find out if you're crap in the sack– you have to find out now. Before anyone's had the chance to catch their breath,

unload as many questions as you can. Was that good? Did you come? Are you sure? Was it the best you've ever had and, if not, who was better and what can I do in the future to claim the top spot? No time for cuddling or enjoying the intimacy, just get her to answer your questions right now.

It's over, isn't it?

You had your shot and you ruined it, and although your partner is assuring you that she had a great time, you're pretty sure that right now she's sick of the sight of you and just wants you out of the house. And if she doesn't want you out of the house, she will shortly because you're about to ask her the same list of performance questions again, just to be sure.

Press the matter again at a later date

Maybe tomorrow, maybe next week. Maybe every day or after every time you go to bed together. Sex, then a survey. Refer to it as an 'exit poll' – that's funny. Make her laugh, even if you can't make her come.

FOOD PREPARATION

AN IRISH DELI WORKER'S GUIDE TO MAKING A ROLL

PREPARING a roll for starving lunch breakers can be one of the most important positions a person can have in society; you're responsible for their mid-work nutrients and are thus one of, if not *the* most important people in their lives. Such is the vital nature of this role, *WWN* has put together a handy guide to preparing this key source of sustenance.

Quotes of The Year

'I've no idea what I'm doing.'
- Enoch Burke

Ask the customer what they want but never listen to the answer
Listening to what the customer wants is a big no-no in deli-roll making. You're not a bar person who can take several drinks orders at once without making a mistake, you're an Irish deli worker and there are standards to adhere to. Ask them what they'd like in their roll before cutting the roll and asking them again several more times with each ingredient. This way you'll always get the order of the ingredients wrong.

Put the protein in last so it flops out when opened
Ham, chicken, beef, whatever the fucking meat is – just make sure it's on top of all the other poorly misplaced items in the customer's roll. At seven quid a pop, they'll love you for it. Why not put the grated cheese in first while you're at it? Or if they're meat-free, leave the lettuce until last so it spills all over the place. Whatever you do, never make a deli roll for a customer like you're making it for yourself. Leave all logic at home with your morals.

Plaster the roll in butter
Train your ear to ignore the request 'just a tiny bit please', as this could contribute to your customer's good health. This should also be the case for mayo, southwest sauce, sweet chilli sauce, and all other condiments that will cause a saggy-ass roll. Cake that shit on like there's no tomorrow and no detrimental health consequences.

Never ask if they want anything else before swiftly moving on to the next customer
Obviously.

URBAN LIVING

HERE'S HOW ALL YOUR OLD HAUNTS HAVE FARED SINCE YOU LEFT TOWN 10 YEARS AGO

BEEN away from home for a while? Maybe you emigrated in the late 2000s? Or maybe you've been living in another county for work/marriage/legal reasons. Either way, you're back in your hometown for the weekend with a bit of a thirst on you, so let's see how your old locals are doing.

Predictions for 2024

Leo Varadkar will become so advanced he'll be indistinguishable from AI.

The majority of pubs in the town are now shut

It's hard for you to believe, but only a few of your old haunts are still open. For a moment, you pause to wonder just how much drink you and the lads must have put away back in the day,

Dictionary Additions of 2024

'Varadcare': the ability to be completely emotionally flat no matter how harrowing the circumstances, for example, the record homeless figures.

given that your departure from the town seems to have single-handedly shut down pubs that were open for decades beforehand.

The local nightclub is now a discount supermarket

All nightlife in the town seems to end at midnight, even on a Friday night. The nightclub that everyone used to swarm to is shut, leaving you to question where exactly young people go these days to drink and shift and fight? Your parents always spoke of how the dancehalls they grew up with vanished overnight, but you

never thought this would happen to the nightclubs you loved. You gave this place the best years of your life.

At least there are still fights

Your favourite pub is now a bookies and your trusty nightclub is now a direct provision hub. Your chips are healthier and it's somehow harder to get a taxi than it was 20 years ago when there were thousands on the streets, but at least it's reassuring to know that you can still get your head kicked in if you look at the wrong fucker sideways. Some things never change.

FAMILY

GIVING OUT TO EVERYONE THE SECOND YOU GET HOME FROM WORK

WORK is always so stressful – the commute, the people, the financial worries of everyday life – so what better way to release all that pent-up anger than offloading everything onto your loved ones in the hopes they'll someday understand how much they mean to you through the medium of irate interactions.

First, upon your arrival home, make a beeline for the kitchen in the hopes there's a little bit of a mess to get things going. Fuck the entire household out of it over an upside-down mug in the sink or a soggy teabag on the counter, before lecturing your spouse or children about how 'no one does anything around here'. They'll love you even more for being so straight up about how your day went.

Did everyone else in the house have a worse 12 hours than you? Who cares? Your series of stressful events are a priority and your life is key to their existence, so they better not start on about their stupid boss, Sean, they

wouldn't know a bad day if it beeped at them in a 2023 Range Rover Sport.

Once you're satisfied your better half is now as miserable as you, move onto your kids, starting from the top down. Responsibility lies at the top tier, so make sure to hold the eldest to task for their younger siblings' failings. If your family is not on high alert the second you come home, then you're failing as a parent.

Once you've finally settled down for the evening, you can now chillax, become all nice and friendly, and then wonder why your entire family

is ignoring you. This is the perfect opportunity to throw a strop and head to bed for a little cry.